NO SWASTIKAS IN SOUTHBURY

NO SWASTIKAS IN SOUTHBURY

MELINDA K. ELLIOTT

AMERICA
THROUGH TIME®
ADDING COLOR TO AMERICAN HISTORY

To all those
who save the bits and pieces of life
which later becomes our only link to history.

America Through Time® is an imprint of Sutton Publishing Inc.
www.through-time.com
office@through-time.com

First published 2023
Reprinted 2025

ISBN 978-1-63499-447-7

Typeset in 10pt on13pt Sabon
Printed and bound in England

Foreword

Since first delving into the history of how Southbury thwarted the German-American Bund's effort to establish a camp our town in 1937, I have known that here is a story that needs to be told. At a time when so many others opted to look away, led by educated and fair-minded clergy and crafty officials, here were townspeople rallying together to successfully fight against Nazism. Nearly lost until recent years, thanks to several champions that basic narrative is now widely celebrated within and far beyond our community, including at the United States Holocaust Memorial Museum.

Yet to fully appreciate what happened, it must be examined in all its complexity. Invariably, as strengths and weaknesses are exposed, the characters will prove messier—and perhaps greater. This is precisely what Melinda Elliott offers us in this well-researched account, as she introduces us to a cast of small-town folk striving to do the right thing. Detailing their circumstances and decision-making, we see individuals and a town opting to confront an alarming and no longer distant evil. In so doing, they offer us a model activism and empathy.

This book serves as an invaluable resource, and most welcomed addition, to the growing body of work about Southbury's unique protest against Nazi indoctrination. Enjoy, and be inspired by the heroism recounted.

Rabbi Eric Polokoff
B'nai Israel of Southbury

Acknowledgments

During this five-year project, many people helped me along the way. Even my grandchildren were pressed into being research assistants, proofreaders, or transcribers of articles. At this point, they may know as much about the subject as I do.

As with any historical research, we learn about a subject based on observations and writing from others who came before us. I offer a special thanks to those who collected and saved information about the Bund incident in Southbury. The real heroes are the families who donated primary source material to the Southbury Historical Society museum, especially the collections from the Lindsay, Hicock, and Hinman families. Also incredibly helpful were the town residents who openly shared photos, scrapbooks, and stories about their relatives who were part of the story.

A special thanks is extended to the staff of the *Waterbury Republican American* who were integral in the keeping Southbury aware of what was happening in almost real time through their daily newspaper installments. And for their generous permission to use the original photographs from 1937.

But most of all, I appreciate the numerous encouragers. Many cheerleaders (especially my husband) kept me going with their excitement about the book and their confidence that I could do the story justice. My family tops the list in this category. They offered me kind words, extreme patience and advice. Their best advice was to "keeping going and don't put the manuscript into the shredder."

Contents

INTRODUCTION

"We Want No Swastikas"

If a story is never told, it becomes something else ... forgotten.
Tatiana de Rosnay

How does a symbol bring out our emotions and become an object of honor or hate?

We will never forget the multitude of American flags that flew across the hills and dales of America after the 9/11 attack in 2001. Or the feelings of pride, bravery, honor, hope, and confidence we felt when viewing the stars and stripes.

So why do other symbols bring out different emotions? How can an object produce a swelling of pride or a burst of fear? The emotion depends on the history and memories we assigned to it.

One day a youngster arrived in the Old Town Hall Museum with his mother. The school assignment was to visit a museum and answer a short survey. This was not what the young teenager wanted to do. Obviously, a museum was a boring place to go with nothing of interest for a middle-schooler. He stood with arms across his chest and leaned against the wall, face hidden by a hoodie. His mom walked around looking at the displays and making comments. A sudden gasp turned all heads to look at the boy. "A swastika!" he exclaimed. He had spotted a small swastika in the corner of a map across the room. He went over to the display about the German-American Bund and read through the whole thing. The student was immediately drawn into a moment of local history and asked a lot of questions. For a middle-schooler, the swastika was a symbol of curiosity, of danger, or something forbidden.

On another day, an elderly man entered the museum with a donation. As he told the story of his item, the man glanced across the room. His gaze froze and he stopped mid-sentence and became very still. He was lost in a momentary trance when his whole body began to shake. Taking a deep breath, he apologized. "I'm sorry. The swastika..." He did not have to finish his statement. There was no doubt the symbol carried a deeply painful meaning for him.

A symbol carries the thoughts, impressions, and history of what the viewer's background brings to it. To a child, a swastika is just a symbol seen in textbooks. But to a person who has lived through a horror, the same symbol becomes a crippling moment as a reminder of fear and terror.

Why is such a symbol in a small museum in Southbury, Connecticut?

In 1937, the German-American Bund, a pro-Nazi organization, secretly purchased land in Southbury to build a camp based on the Hitler Youth camps of Nazi Germany. The town of less than 1,300 residents decided to stop the camp. Even though the atrocities of World War II were yet to happen, hatred and oppression were already attached to the swastika.

While Southbury may have seemed like an isolated little town that knew nothing of the world, that is far from the truth. Many of the townsfolk were highly educated at Ivy League universities. Others were veterans of the world war and stayed aware of the politics and world news. The residents remained well-informed through local and national newspapers, magazines, the radio, and news reels.

If the German-American Bund thought the town would be a welcoming place to build a camp and a German community, they did not understand the underlying strength of Yankee tenacity.

Miss Jennie Hinman said it very well: "We want no swastika or any other flag to fly here but the American Flag. We want no part of this community devoted to teaching young Americans a philosophy that is contrary to the ideals of democracy for which our people fought and for which we will stand today. This is not exactly good ground for the Nazi idea."

1

Nothing Ever Happens in Southbury

Southbury, Connecticut

"NOTHING interesting has ever happened here," is a statement that makes local historians cringe. However, any town surviving over 300 years has been the setting for dramas, mysteries, and intrigues. Since the settlers first arrived, Southbury has seen everything from grave robbers, scandals, gambling, murder, the Ku Klux Klan, mayhem, bootlegging, and a Nazi invasion.

Southbury began as part of Pomperaug Plantation in 1673, as a frontier settlement with fifteen families arriving from Stratford. After a year, the plantation became a town and was named Woodbury. Through the years, more land was needed for the crops and housing. The town expanded south to form the Southbury Parish in 1731, and a church was built. In 1766, the Parish of South Britain was started.[1]

During the Revolutionary War, the town hosted General George Washington and General Rochambeau as they traveled through the area. Southbury contributed meat, grain and clothing to the rebel troops throughout the war. They also sent sons and fathers to serve as soldiers in the battles of Ticonderoga and White Plains.

Twelve years after the war Southbury registered as a town separating from Woodbury in 1787. The new town included both parishes of Southbury and South Britain.

The meeting houses were the center of both communities. The white-spired, unheated buildings were used for worship services twice each Sunday. There was a state religion at this time, and all the residents were expected to attend. Between the services, the nearby Sabbath house nearby provided a warm place to eat lunch. Normal work was forbidden on Sundays, according to state law.

The all-resident annual town meeting happened every December on a Tuesday afternoon and alternated yearly between the two parishes. A town meeting was where business, elections and important issues was discussed and voted on. Anyone was allowed to speak, for as long and as often as they wanted. Every viewpoint was heard and discussed before the gathering came to an acceptable conclusion.

A special town meeting could be called at any time, with a seven-day notice. Such a meeting was held in February 1819, to find a way to prevent and punish people who were removing corpses from fresh graves.[2] The most recent body snatch was the remains of a town war hero. Medical students were often in need of cadavers and looked for fresh burials, especially during the winter. At their special town meeting, Southbury voted to offer a $100 reward to anyone with information that would lead to punishment of the offenders.

Education was always a priority in Southbury. The first school was established in 1741. Later, additional school districts were established with a one-room school house in each. The schools were named for their section of town, including White Oak, Bullet Hill, Southford, South Britain, Kettletown, Pierce Hollow, and The Purchase.

In the early 1800s, small industries and farms supplied all the local needs. The town flourished with fertile farmland and good grazing land for sheep and cattle. Mills and small industries were set up along all the Pomperaug River, and the Eight-Mile Brook running along the borders. Other small brooks provided power for tools and supplies needed.

The railroad officials choose Southbury for its trans-state route between Danbury to Hartford directly through the full width of the town. The transportation expanded the market place to transport products and people to larger cities. New factories were built and additional industries came to town. The town's population continue to grow, as more factory workers were needed.

Eventually, the nearby cities of Waterbury and Naugatuck built giant, modern factory buildings, creating a need for a large number of workers. Many of the Southbury laborers moved to the higher paying jobs in the cities. At the same time, other residents left Southbury in wagon trains to find new land and new beginnings in the west.

Southbury went from being a busy industrial center, to a quieter town with a rural life style. Many Irish immigrants who worked on the railroad decided to settle in Southbury. A number Lithuanian and German dairy farmers bought the abandoned farmlands in the high hills of the Purchase district. An artisan community was established by Count Ilya Tolstoy and George Grebenstchikoff on a hillside overlooking the Housatonic River. They called the community Russian Village. The 1930 census shows that 32 percent of Southbury households were foreign born. The majority were German, followed by Lithuanian, Irish, and Polish.

The state religion was discontinued, and the meeting houses became congregational churches. New houses of worship were built to provide for the needs of the residents, and especially the immigrants. Even into the twentieth century, the elected town leaders predominantly came from the congregational church.

A number of Southbury men were soldiers who fought in World War I. After the war, many were able to find construction jobs on the Stevenson dam in Oxford. The Housatonic River was harnessed to supply electricity for the factories down the river. In creating Lake Zoar, several Southbury houses and farms were flooded. A group of industrious men salvaged wood and building supplies from the condemned houses and built the Community House for an activity and meeting center.

The higher water level made the primary bridge between Newtown and Southbury unusable and it was torn down. This left only one crossing; a wooden-planked bridge that connected to Sandy Hook's Glen Road.

The new waterfront at Lake Zoar created a recreation area for boating and fishing. Sections of land near the river were subdivided into small lots of 25 by 50 feet. For $25, a family could own a piece land big enough to pitch a tent or make a camping shack to enjoy the summer near the water. Housing developers jumped at the opportunity to build miniature neighborhoods. Among these were Cedarland, Oakdale Manor, the Berkshires, and Lakeside.

Lakeside had prime land along Lake Zoar along a secluded cove. The developers, Soule and Roberts constructed cottages with running water and electricity. The settlement was well-advertised around the tristate area as a "Restricted Summer Colony," and a "Christian Community." This was not uncommon. The clear understanding at the time meant, "No Jews or Negros" were welcomed.[3]

During this decade, there was a resurgence of the Ku Klux Klan in Connecticut. The Northern version of the Klan was not racial or violent like the Southern KKK during the Civil War. The new Klan stood for "100 percent Americanism" against immigrants, especially Catholics and Jews, who were perceived as taking away jobs from the Americans. In the 1920s, the Klan had 65,000 members in Connecticut.[4]

Southburians were split in support of the KKK and those against. This caused bitter feelings between friends. One night, a fiery cross was burned in a ceremony at Sand corner with hundreds of hooded Klan members in attendance. The local Klansmen tried to control the politics, but the movement only lasted three or four years.[5]

Prohibition did not stop the locals from making their own hard cider. The Oak Tree Inn kept their stash of liquor in a nearby ancient root cellar, protected by a heavy oak door. It appeared to be a tomb, with the inscription, "Here lies John Barleycorn, died July 1, 1919, RIP." But this did not fool the State Police who recovered 23 cases of beer and 16 barrels of hard cider during a raid.[6]

In 1930, the pastors in South Britain realized several families came to church on Sundays without the head of their family. After a quick investigation, the problem was found. A weekly craps game at a local dairy barn was enticing men and boys away from the church. After a quiet word to the constable and a very public arrest of prominent citizens, the errant men returned to the fold.[7]

A turning point for the town came when the State Highway Department chose Southbury as part of the major inland east-west route through the state. Designated as Route 6, this roadway was destined to become the second largest road system through the state, second only to the Post Road along the coast. A stronger, wider bridge was planned to replace the Victorian bridge originally built for horse and carriage traffic. The road through town was improved and paved in order to become a state highway. Southbury residents watched as the construction progressed, giving them time to prepare for the new wave of visitors.

With the expected increase of automobiles, dozens of gas stations, and restaurants sprang up along State Route 6 to cater to any budget. For a low cost option, the local farm stands sold fresh produce, cheese, and baked goods provided by the farmer's wife. And for those who needed a place to spend the night, small hotels and inns were readily available.

Nellie Brown opened a small restaurant with only four tables serving home-grown and locally sourced food. Her successful chicken pot pie at the "Old Hundred" encouraged her to expand the restaurant. She needed to add additional chicken coops, keeping plenty of hens available for dinners. In the first year alone, ten thousand people were served at Old Hundred.[8]

While grateful for the business, Southbury's main road became congested through town especially on weekends. Reports of hour-long traffic jams were not uncommon. More than one car left the road looking for an alternate route and got stuck in the mud along the unpaved farm paths. In spite of this, celebrities, writers, doctors and lawyers were drawn to this rural area, as it was close enough to New York to visit over the weekends and far enough away to leave the busy world behind.

2
Der Hitler

Americans first learned about Adolf Hitler in 1922. A *New York Times* article warned that Hitler and his anti-Semitic movement could become dangerous, however, it was not at this time.[1]

Hitler became the leader of the National Socialist Party in 1920, two years after he became a member. The group's name was changed to the National Socialist Worker's Party—the Nazis. Their symbol, the swastika, would become the most hated symbol in modern history.

As the leader of the fledgling Nazi organization, Hitler was a dynamic speaker. In his tirades against Jews, Communists, and the Treaty of Versailles, Hitler attracted large crowds. His rage against the treatment of Germany after the war was shared by the audience.

The Allies blamed the Germans for starting World War I and gave out stiff punishments in the Treaty of Versailles. The Germans were ordered to reimburse the countries they invaded to compensate their monetary loses. All of the German weapons of war had to be destroyed, and they were allowed a small military force for protection. The Germans were also required to apologize for the war. The embarrassed country riled against the blame and punishment. As they strained to pay the reparation bills, the average citizen struggled to heat his house and put food on the table.

Hitler promised his followers he could lead a powerful government with law and order. Under his leadership, every person would have a job and food. He asked everyone to commit to work hard toward the goal. Together, they would make Germany a world power.

As Hitler's popularity increased, his statements became bolder. He called for the Germanic people to return to their ancient roots of pure Aryan descent. He said Germany was polluted with outsiders who diluted the pure bloodline. This needed to be cleansed, because the Aryans were the superior race. Hitler claimed the Jewish influence was the root of all social and moral evil. Hitler demanded this evil be eliminated.

Hitler defined the primary goal of the country was to gain *Lebensraum*—living space—for the master race: the Aryans. He stated Aryans' destiny was to conquer the world. Their first step was to reclaim the lands Germany had to return in the Treaty of Versailles.

The Nazis started a uniformed private security group, called the SA (*Sturmabteilung*)—also known as the Stormtroopers and Brownshirts. Their alleged mission was to protect the citizens from violence during the speeches. Soon they were armed with blackjacks and pistols as they marched in the streets, starting brawls and exerting their power.

Wilhelm Murr, a Nazi politician, claimed that the Nazis did not say "an eye for an eye, a tooth for a tooth." He said: "Anyone who knocks out one of our teeth will get his jaw bashed in." The SA became increasingly aggressive, breaking up meetings of communist and other organizations.[2]

Hitler attempted to overthrow the government in the 1923. This became known as the Munich Putsch. The venture was unsuccessful and Hitler ended up in jail. While there, he had time to clarify his thoughts on how to gain nationwide power. He revealed his goals in his book, *Mein Kampf*. The new plan would win power through the democratic system by legal means, and not through violence. Hitler wanted absolute power, but he was willing to take it in stages and wait for the right timing.

In 1930, Hitler told an American reporter that German minds were full of chaos and confusion. They were discouraged by debts, taxes, unemployment, and the current government. The remedy was hope, order, prosperity, and purpose. He was determined to become the savior of the Germanic people and lead them out of the chaos. Hitler's plan was to keep Germany free from foreign powers who could economically enslave them.[3]

Hitler's inner circle of leaders faithfully provided the framework to carry out his ideas. The country was enticed by Hitler's message of becoming a super nation, and willingly obeyed his party's views. The Nazi party continued to gather followers and power.

In January 1933, Adolf Hitler was appointed chancellor of Germany. He told the citizens his goal was peace, but within a month, he informed his military leaders to prepare for war. Hitler began making dramatic changes in the country. First, he became absolute leader of the country through a decree of emergency power. This allowed him to imprison enemies without a trial and to restrict free speech. He also made laws without government approval. Soon, Hitler removed any opposition to his plans by banning all other political parties. In a vote that followed, the Nazis won the legal right to run the government.

As promised, the Nazis party provided work for the German men, but not the way anyone imagined. Men from all occupations were forced to work on building roads, factories, and laying the groundwork for war. They were not given a choice; the unions were banned and any talk of striking was punishable by death.

Thirteen concentration camps were built in 1933 by the laborers. These were used to house political prisoners or anyone the Nazis wanted to punish. When the Jehovah Witnesses refused to swear an oath to Hitler, they were rounded up and taken to the camps.

The Nazis began to regiment the thought of all Germans. Instead of regional greetings, a new national one was introduced. All residents were required to raise their right hand, while saying "*Heil* Hitler." Anything or anyone that could influence free thought was systematically destroyed. Within 100 days of Hitler's coming to power, books with a philosophy other than his own were burned in massive bonfires.

The Nazis set out to indoctrinate all residents, by aligning their thoughts and actions with Hitler's ideas and ideals. His philosophies became the rules of everyday life. All aspects were dictated on what to read, what to wear, and what to think. There was no privacy. Personal conversations could be reported to the police, and even letters and correspondence were subject to censorship.

The government took over the newspapers and radio stations broadcasting only approved Nazi content. All other opinions were banned. To make sure each family could listen to the latest propaganda messages, inexpensive radios were built and distributed, which only received channels from approved stations.[4] Entertainment and cultural programs were intermixed with national propaganda messages. Anything broadcast had to glorify Hitler or the Nazis.

Churches and religious organizations did not meet Hitler's standard of approved Nazi content. Pastors were banned from preaching the Bible. Consequently, many were dragged from the pulpit by the Stormtroopers and sent to labor camps. At first, the Catholic Church had an agreement with the Nazis to continue on undisturbed, but it was not long before hundreds of priests and nuns were beaten and imprisoned for long stretches.

Women's roles were strictly limited. Their professional jobs were eliminated and they were sent home to take care of their families. The women were given strict advice on running a Nazi home, including instructions on house cleaning and approved meals to cook.

One Sunday each month, the whole nation ate *Einstopf* for dinner. This one-pot meal was made from inexpensive local ingredients.[5] The money saved from the frugal dinner was collected for the *Wintershilfswerk*—a Nazi fund to help the veterans and poor survive the winter.

German farmers were glorified for providing meat, vegetables, and grains, making the country almost self-sustaining. Under Nazi supervision, they planted the crops they were told to grow, or their land would be taken away. Impossibly strict production goals were placed on the farmers to produce larger yields from their crops. The whole country helped out by saving table scraps to feed the pigs.

Even the children had to follow Nazi rules. Beginning in kindergarten, they learned from Nazified books to hate the Jews and worship Hitler. Songs with propaganda messages and catchy tunes were sung until the hidden messages were imbedded into their minds. The children were no longer innocent individuals, but part of a collective.

Recreation time for children was rigorously controlled. The children's clubs and camps were closed, and the Nazis established the Hitler Youth program. Physical activity and strict obedience to their leaders were of vital importance. Wearing uniforms removed all class distinction and the youth became standardized in their looks and thinking. Hitler called the youth the future soldiers of the nation. Training for the Hitler Youth, and the German Youngsters for younger boys, included outdoor activities, sports, parading, and war games. Each day, they recited an oath to the swastika flag and Hitler: "In the presence of this banner, which represents our Fuhrer, I swear to devote all my energies and my strength to the savior of our country, Adolf Hitler. I am willing and ready to give up my life for him, so help me God."

In order to purify the country for the Aryans, Hitler composed a statement that explicitly explained who was a citizen of the new regime, and who was not. Those excluded were the gypsies, Communists, and Jews.

Jews were forced out of government positions and were subjected to public humiliation. The Nazis imposed a boycott of Jewish-owned businesses, which was crippling to their communities. Jewish children were forced out of the public schools.

Meanwhile, Hitler secretly created new military forces, war machines, and ammunition right under the nose of the Allies, tripling the size allowed in the Treaty of Versailles.

The next year, in 1934, Hitler assumed the additional role of the president after the death of President Hindenburg. Adolf Hitler now has absolute power over Germany.

The international newspapers were increasingly full of news in Nazi Germany. America watched as the Germans gave away their freedoms in exchange for a dream of a strong country and a nation free of impurities of race or philosophies. The Germans were becoming one race, and one country united under one leader: Adolf Hitler.

3

Those American Nazis

From the very beginning of the National Socialist Worker's Party, Adolf Hitler had an ultimate plan of world domination. Nazi party members were discreetly sent to America and other countries to gather information. The first wave arrived in America in 1923. Some entered with student visas and others crossed at the Mexican border. Their purpose was to locate dams, factories, and military bases, and the observers sent detailed reports and maps to the Nazi leaders in Germany, supplying a list of resources available in America.

The second wave of Nazis settled in America to form cell groups and build a Nazi framework. They met with the established German communities to persuade the groups to learn about the Nazi regime under Hitler. Within a few years, the Chicago area cells combined to begin the Society of Teutonia, led by Fritz and Peter Gissibl. This was the first organization to openly support the Nazis in the United States. Soon after, German officers were sent to train the members in marching and drilling.

When Germany led an economic boycott against the Jewish-owned businesses, Americans called for a boycott of German goods. Rabbi Stephen S. Wise stated that what was happening in Germany today may happen tomorrow in any other land. He encouraged people to speak out.

Anti-Nazi protest marches were held in at least sixty-five American cities. In Philadelphia, 20,000 men protested in the streets. While in Chicago, over 50,000 men marched through town even though a large group of Nazis lived there. At the same time, hundreds of thousands of protest petitions were signed and sent to the government.

As Hitler gathered more backing and power in Germany, the American Nazi groups grew larger and bolder. The numerous cells battled for power and recognition from Germany. Heinz Spanknoebel, a member of the Detroit cell, announced he had authority from German authorities to become the Nazi leader of the United States. Spanknoebel said his orders were to name the organization the Friends of New Germany. Other tasks included enforcing the leadership principle of absolute obedience.

Spanknoebel declared that all German organizations in America, Nazi or not, had to answer to him. He began to form drill units of the *Sturmabteilung*, the Stormtroopers. Spanknoebel tried to emulate Hitler in speech, looks, and actions, and he ordered violence and intimidation as a means of control.

The Friends of New Germany were organized into three geographic divisions across the States. These were the Eastern, the Middle West, and the Western divisions.

Each region had their own elected leader who reported directly to Spanknoebel. To join the Friends of New Germany, an applicant was required to pledge an oath to Hitler and promise to obey the people over them by uniform or by power status. Also required was a list names and addresses of family members still in Germany. The unspoken threat implied the member must do what the Friends demanded, or their German family would suffer retribution.

The Friends of New Germany established Youth Camps in seventeen locations to get the children out into the fresh air. Several were very small or temporary campsites. The camps operated much as any other camps with hiking, boating, and singing. The difference was these camps were conducted in German and taught Nazi philosophies. The children saluted the Swastika and swore an oath to their Great Leader, Adolf Hitler.

Camp Siegfried was started in 1935 as the largest permanent camp site. The camp brought in thousands of campers during the week and trainloads of visitors on weekends and for special events.

The Nazi Organizations Abroad (*Auslanders*) division was created in Germany to control the Nazis groups around the world. These included Nazi organizations in America, Great Britain, Czechoslovakia, Canada, and Argentina. The division office under Ernst Wilhelm Bohle released a statement saying that Germans in any part of the world still came under the German laws and Hitler's authority, even if they did not belong to the Nazi Party.

In March and April 1934, *Today* magazine published a series of articles by Samuel Duff McCoy. The titles were shocking to the American public: "Nazi Invasion of the U. S. Feared" and "Hitlerism Invades America." His well-researched and documented reports proved the Nazis had been in America for many years with the ultimate goal of taking over the country. As a result, the Friends of New Germany and other German groups were under close scrutiny by the public and the government.

That summer, Congressman Samuel Dickstein received over 2,000 letters protesting the Youth Camp Wille und Macht (Will and Power). The camp, located near Princeton, New Jersey, received both local and national censure. Dickstein secretly visited the camp and found large swastika flags flying next to a 4-inch American flag.

Congressman Dickstein was propelled to action after what he had seen. The expansion of youth camps, the violent behavior of the Friends of New Germany, and wide-spread distribution of Nazi propaganda needed to be stopped. As chairman of the committee on Immigration of the House of Representatives, he demanded an investigation into the pro-Nazi activities in the United States. Dickstein, along with Congressman John McCormack of Massachusetts, led the investigations. The inquiries led to the indictment of Heinz Spanknoebel for working as an unregistered foreign agent. He fled the country before he had to appear in court.

The investigations still continued in spite of Spanknoebel's departure. While interviewing Fritz Gissibl, former leader of the Teutonic Society, Congressman

McCormack asked: "Do you still consider Hitler the leader of the German people?"

"Of the German race," Gissibl answered. "Of German blood where found, in Germany and outside."[1]

The leader of the Wille und Macht, Hugo Haas, was also called to testify during the investigation. He said: "There is only one leader, and that is Adolf Hitler. His ideas are our ideas, and his ideals are our ideals." He also added that he felt Americans needed to learn from Germany and adopt Nazi reforms.

Congressman Dickstein established an ongoing investigation group that would later be known as the House Committee on Un-American Activities.

The anti-Nazi turmoil was brought to Adolf Hitler's attention. He did not need any extra scrutiny from America while he was in the process of violating Germany's agreement with the Allies. His government decreed that members of the Nazi party could not belong to the Friends of New Germany. Many of the members and leaders left the group. Some returned to Germany and to serve directly under Hitler.

4
Reverend Lindsay is Worried

Southbury, Connecticut

Reverend M. Edgar N. Lindsay tossed the booklet onto his desk, not wanting to believe what he had just read. Adolf Hitler, the leader of Germany, was systematically closing churches, arresting their pastors, and throwing them into jail.

Rev. Lindsay had no reason to doubt the resolution, "American Churches to Hitler," published by the American Federal Council of the Churches. They accused Hitler of teaching and glorifying hate as a basic virtue.[1] Hate as a basic virtue? How can that be?

The booklet claimed Hitler's message was spreading throughout Germany, of "explicitly teaching and urging hate-hate-hate." It was echoed in newspapers, and written into the books for the schoolrooms.

Lindsay mulled over the article's distressful warning. "What is happening in Germany is not just of local significance, but of importance the world over." Surely this could not be the future of American churches, too.

Reverend Lindsay looked out at the quaint village of South Britain, nestled in a valley under the spires of the old meeting house. In 1766, the residents were allowed to meet there in the winter, avoiding the dangerous drive over the mountain, to attend meetings at the Southbury Meeting House. The iconic white church was built in 1825.

Lindsay fell in love with the town when he arrived in 1929, as a Yale Divinity student. Born and raised in Virginia, he brought a bit of Southern charm to this New England town of 1,300 residents. Right away, he realized he needed to tread carefully and kindly, to allow time for the parishioners to trust him. They were confused and cautious, because the previous pastor left after only nine months.

Pastor Oliver William could not connect with the staid New Englanders. His modern and radical ideas were too hard for them to accept. Pastor William's membership in the Socialist Party simply rubbed the people the wrong way and he was never able to gain the respect of the conservative congregation.[2]

Rev. Lindsay worked hard to promote healing and refocus his flock to Godly activities. Glancing down at the booklet brought him back to the immediate problem. He prayed that Hitler's brand of hate would never come to his congregation.

A son of Southbury raised a red flag about the Nazis in 1934 when he published a book called *Nazi Means War*. Leland Stowe served as a foreign journalist in Berlin and had first-hand knowledge of the rise of Hitler. When his book was released, he was kicked out of Germany.

Even though Rev. Lindsay was aware of the threat of Nazism in American, he was unaware it was already nearby.

Stamford, Connecticut

The Friends of New Germany were ready to expand their influence and their pro-Nazi philosophies. Connecticut was the perfect location for new recruits, as it was the gateway to New England, and near New York with the hub of Nazi activities.

The first step was to locate Germans settlements. As with most immigrants, the Germans were a close-knit community that would get together to share their common language, culture, and foods. The Friends member would attended meetings of the German club or organizations, and explain the benefits the Nazi Party could offer their group.

The first Connecticut Friends of New Germany unit was established in Stamford, a town very close to New York City. As the group grew, they were encouraged to branch out into the state to establish new units.

Speakers from the Stamford units were sent out to visit the German communities in the cities of New Haven, Waterbury, Danbury, and Bridgeport, hoping to establish cell groups.

One enthusiastic speaker, Wolfgang T. Jung, went to Southbury to meet with the German immigrants. He returned several times and invited them to meetings in Stamford and New York. One man, whose parents were of German descent, remembered attending the meetings with his parents as a young boy. Looking back, he realized that the Nazis represented evil. But as a child, he did not see anything wrong with the meetings.

Wolfgang Jung's report to his unit was very positive. A new cell group was being contemplated in Southbury.

The Friends of New Germany followed the pattern of Nazi Youth Camps for camps. Camp Efdende in Detroit was one of the earliest endeavors and Camp Siegfried in Yaphank, Long Island, opened in 1935. The other Friends camps were located in Cleveland, Philadelphia, Chicago, Buffalo, Los Angeles, and Portland, Oregon.

Camp Siegfried was a great success. Situated on 40 acres of land outside of Yaphank, Long Island, it was currently the largest Bund camp in the nation. During the summer, the camp housed a total of 1,000–1,500 youth a week. A special train was added to the Long Island railroad to bring in visitors directly to the camp. On special occasions, 15,000 people were expected to attend. Photographs of the event with children saluting the swastika and marching in formation appeared in the newspapers.

Deciding that it was time to make a move, the Stamford Unit voted to begin the process of building a camp in Connecticut.

5
German-American Bund

After the loss of their leader, Heinz Spanknoebel, the Friends of New Germany continued with various leaders for over a year. At a conference on March 1936 in Buffalo, New York, Fritz Julius Kuhn was elected to take over the declining organization.

The first item on Kuhn's agenda was to change the focus of the group. He recommended making it into an American group and formed the *Amerikadeutche Volksbund*; known in English as the German-America Bund. Only American citizens, either natural born or naturalized, could belong to the group. Little else changed from the old Friends of New Germany group. The German foreign minister claimed they are the same people, with the same principles, and the same appearance.[1]

The German-American Bund grew quickly under Kuhn's leadership because of his organizational skills. He developed new companies under the umbrella of the Bund. The first three were the German-American Business League, the A.V. Publishing Corporation, and the A.V. Development Corporation. The "A.V." represented the first letter of the *Amerikadeutche Volksbund*. Other businesses would include the German-American Settlement League and various newspapers in German and English. Kuhn was officially the head of all the business. Proceeds from the companies went directly into the Bund's bank accounts.

The Bund helped German-American families during the Depression. A Women's Auxiliary was formed to help women and families. Also, an American version of the *Wintershilfswerk*, or Winter Work, charity was created to raise funds to feed the poor. The Bund provided companionship, fed the families that were hungry, developed jobs for those who needed them, and provided gathering places.

While it was nice to be fed and protected by the Bund, the price was obedience. Bund members were told where to shop and given lists of the approved businesses, and these merchants had to pay a mandatory tax to the Bund to be included.

The German-American Bund appeared to be a group under the direct control of Adolf Hitler. The Bund held rallies filled with Nazi salutes, German songs, and "*Heil* Hitlers." The swastika flag was carried next to the American flag by men in Nazi-like uniforms. Bund leaders gave scathing speeches warning of the Jews and Communists taking over America. The German-American Bund pledged to fight for their adopted country. Fritz Kuhn said the Bund is determined to fight for Americanism, and anyone who did not agree with the Bund was considered a Jew or under Jewish influence.

Fritz Kuhn asked Bund members to raise funds to send a large delegation to Berlin for the 1936 Summer Olympics. At the same time, money was collected for a donation to the *Wintershilfswerk*. Over 6,000 members contributed to the funds. They were allowed to write their name and a message on pages that were later bound into *The Golden Book of American Germandom* to be presented to Hitler. Inside the book cover was an inscription that included:

> In America, the hearts of the German people also beat for the great leader of all Germans. Thousands upon thousands have found new hope and faith through him and his work. The German-American Bund is the expression of his National Socialist worldview.[2]

Over 200 Bundist traveled together to Germany. The day after they arrived in Germany, a group of uniformed members were invited to participate in a march with Hitler's storm troopers. Immediately afterward, Kuhn and four of his leaders were received by Adolf Hitler. *The Golden Book* was handed to *Der Führer*, along with a hefty envelop for the *Wintershilfswerk*. After posing for photographs, the group was escorted out, allowing the next waiting group to enter. As they were leaving, Hitler said: "Go over there and continue the fight."

Carl Nicolay, leader of the Brooklyn unit, had traveled to Germany ahead of the others to prepare for the Bund's visit. Nicolay was invited to stay in Germany longer and speak to groups around the country, and design a presentation to show the Youth Camp's stronghold in America. One day, Edward, duke of Winsor, wandered into an exposition hall and saw Nicolay's exhibition with photographs of the activities at Camp Siegfried and other camps.

In a letter sent to his temporary replacement in Brooklyn, Nicolay wrote: "I had to promise the Hitler Youth Leadership here a lecture before the assembled leaders of the Hitler Youth and League of German Girls before I leave."[3]

While in Germany, Carl Nicolay attended a training course given by the Propaganda Ministry. When he returned to America after being away a year, Nicolay said he was ready to fulfill his mission.[4] He immediately got involved in the plans for the new camp in Connecticut and began scheduling speaking engagements.

6
Camps and Conflicts

Bund Headquarters, New York City, 1937

The photograph of Fritz Kuhn and Adolf Hitler at the Olympics continued to appear in newspapers around the country, and the general public interpreted it as confirmation Kuhn and the German-American Bund received orders directly from the *Führer*. This led to hundreds of new memberships and a surge of energy within the Bund communities.

To harness the momentum, Kuhn encouraged the Bund units to purchase land and sponsor youth camps. By indoctrinating the children with Nazi values in a fun setting away from their parents, the Bund would be guaranteed to continue for many years. The units were urged to sacrifice their money and time to build the camps.

The Bund leadership decided to follow the design of Camp Siegfried in the construction of camps. Two were scheduled to be open in 1937, Camp Nordland, and Camp General von Steuben. Construction on three more camps was planned to begin the following year.

Camp Nordland was scheduled to open in July 1937, and expected to be even larger than Camp Siegfried, on 97 acres of land 5 miles outside of Andover, New Jersey. The town of 479 residents were mostly unaware of the purchase in March 1937, and virtually oblivious to the construction of fifteen cottages.

Invitations for the opening of Camp Nordland were sent out on swastika stationary to 5,000 pro-Nazi followers. The attendants were promised a flag presentation, military display, and a parade of uniformed marchers. The enclosed literature for the Camp Nordland stated it would "be a place which breathes of the spirit of the New Germany." The article claimed the youth would be strengthened and confirmed in National Socialism making them conscious of the role which has been assigned to them as the future carriers of Germans racial ideals in America.[1]

Camp Nordland opened with a large ceremony on July 18, with all the promised fanfare of speakers and marchers, including 100 youth. Fritz Kuhn himself arrived at the camp for the festivities. The crowd was estimated at 10,000 people. After the formalities, everyone was treated to German folk dancing, German food, and German beer.

Almost immediately Representative William M. Citron of Middletown, Connecticut, asked the state and justice departments to investigate the reports the camp would be used as Nazi military training camp. Citron sent letters to Secretary of State Cordell Hull and officials at the Federal Bureau of Investigation with his concerns.[2]

Numerous letters of complaints from New Jersey residents were sent to the local authorities and to their governor. Several veterans and American Legion groups wrote resolutions against the camp, which were also sent to the governor and the newspapers.

The following weekend, neither Camp Siegfried nor Camp Nordland held rallies or marches. Only normal camps activities took place with the children while the adults drank beer. Camp Nordland's leader complained about the hostile reactions of the public, stating they never bothered any other organization and minded their own business. A leader at Camp Siegfried warned the press to "stop picking on us."

Adverse Publicity

The National and local press organizations kept the German-American Bund under close scrutiny.

In August, three national magazines published strong articles warning of the Bund's goals. "Don't Take America for Granted" in *The American Legion Magazine* warned of the growth of sinister influences that might be planning to destroy the American systems.

The Digest simply warned of "Fascism in America," while the most disturbing report was found in the *American* magazine article titled, "An American Fuhrer Organizes an Army." The author Joseph F. Dinneen left no doubt the Bund was controlled by the Nazis and were forming and drilling a secret army. Dinneen claimed they were setting up the infrastructure to eventually take over America. He pointed out the seriousness of the trained and uniformed member was being overlooked by the government.

In September, a Washington, D.C., headline stated, "Nazis Charged With Making '4-H' Propaganda Drive on the U.S." The Bund youth camps were accused of using the 4-Hs of "Health, Hitler, Heils, and Hate" to prevent the Americanization of Bund member's children.[3]

That week, newspaper headlines exploded with fearful titles: "Nazis Plan to Seize U.S. Is Growing;" "Storm Troopers Show Strength at Nazi Rally;" "U.S. Nazis Wield Power Over Diplomats;" and "Charges Nazis Plot to Seize Control." The *Chicago Times* syndicated a series of articles that were carried by newspapers across the country and read by millions. The goal was to expose the inside workings of the German-American Bund, and the graphic photographs of local Nazi rallies of soldiers and uniformed children marching were surprising to most Americans, but especially upsetting were the pictures of the Swastika flag being saluted by children.

The October's *Reader's Digest*, with its wide national readership, featured "Those American Nazis," a condense version of Dinneen's article from the *American* magazine. By then, most people were aware of the German-American Bund and its influence across the nation.

Connecticut, 1937

Meanwhile, plans for the next camp were underway. Wolfgang Jung was tasked with finding a suitable piece of land to build their first camp in western Connecticut. The German-born Jung studied architecture and engineering and moved to America in 1928. He was married and had two children. Jung was involved in the local German Society, along with being a member of the Stamford Bund.

The property for a new camp needed to be within a reasonable driving distance for the sponsoring groups in both Westchester County and Connecticut. Ideally, the new location would be near the proposed new Bund units of Bridgeport, New Haven, Waterbury, and Danbury.

In collaboration with other project officials, Jung spent his spare time with real estate agents to find the perfect piece of land to support both a recreation camp, and a separate youth camp. They were not only were they looking at the camp setting, there were other things to be considered. Besides a large main lodge, space was needed for cabins, a hostel for German youths passing through, and a swimming hole. Ideally, the land would have access to a railway to bring in thousands of people on the weekends.

Real estate agents Bates and Knobloch of Danbury were known for listing large properties and farmland. They had recently worked with the state of Connecticut searching for land to build a campus a "Training School for Mental Defectives."

Realtor Bates knew of a large plot of land would meet all of the Bund's criteria. The acreage was in the Kettletown area of town, named after the land was purchased from the local natives with a copper kettle, plus other compensations. Most recently, the owners kept the land as an investment, but previously it was owned by the Coe Brass factory, also known as the Waterbury Brass Company. The company had cut down the dense forest and shipped the logs to Waterbury where the lumber was used for auxiliary power at the factory.

Wolfgang Jung walked around the property with the agents. It contained plenty of room for the campsite, with running water, very few neighbors, and access to the railroad tracks. Two abandoned roads led to the property, from opposite sides, but neither had been cleared or improved for automobiles. The high meadow off of Georges Hill Road would be perfect for the main lodge, and the rocky out cropping and steep slopes would provide a good hiking route for the children. Not only was the land perfect, the price for the 178 acres was a bargain at just $4,000.

Wolfgang Jung carried out the negotiations with Bates and Knobloch and signed the paperwork for the purchased the land on Saturday, September 25. With the contours of the land in mind, Jung started drawing up plans for the camp buildings.

The nearby Bund units in eastern New York and Stamford combined forces and coordinated their schedules to begin the clearing work at the new campsite. Jung waited until the work dates were set before registering the sale with Southbury Town Hall. He mailed the property deed to the Southbury town clerk on October 25, a full month after the purchase date. Less than two weeks later, the Bund work group of 100 people headed to Southbury to start the preparing the campsite for Camp General von Stueben.

7
First Encounters

November 7, 1937, Sunday

After months of planning, the *Americadeutscher Volksbund* members of Westchester County, New York, and Stamford, Connecticut, were on their way to Southbury to begin the new camp project. The number of workers was fairly impressive for the first day with around 100 people; including men, women, and children.

Thirty-five cars made the trek from various eastern New York locations, following the numerous two-lane roads. At the Lakeside sign in Southbury, the group turned off the main road then up Georges Hill Road. The drive was tough on the rutty dirt road, and after what seemed like miles, the curved road opened up in front of a neat dairy farm. Not knowing exactly where to go from there, many of the Bund members stopped and asked for directions. Dairy farmer David Roulston and his wife pointed the way for the strangers. Their destination was only a short distance farther.

The abandoned road that once led to the Southbury railroad depot was now a narrow path across the meadow, which quickly came to an area covered with white spruce and pine trees. By reopening the old Bullet Hill Road, the Bund would have direct access for special trains to bring large numbers of campers from Danbury and New York. As the cars gathered at the edge of the property, the members were greeted by an enthusiastic Carl "Papa" Nicolay, leader of the Eastern division of the Bund. After words of welcome, Nicolay assigned jobs to the groups of workers. Several were sent to cut down trees, while others cleared away the rocks and stumps for a larger parking area.

The architect of the camp, Wolfgang Jung, proudly showed off his drawing of the camp headquarters and answered questions. He took various leaders to see the area where the main lodge would be constructed, on the hill overlooking the Pomperaug Valley.[1]

After a while, the project treasurer and a camp planner left to locate a place in town to purchase supplies. The clearing and construction projects would take many Sunday work days before the camp would be ready for use. Part of the Bund's goal was to work with the residents of Southbury to form a beneficial relationship. They stopped at the dairy farm to ask David Roulston where to find a store. The Irish farmer sent them down to South Britain to visit a fellow Irishman, Henry McCarthy.

Henry McCarthy saw the black car stop in front of his store of groceries and dry goods. He did not recognize the vehicle, and figured the car was from out of town. Two well-dressed men in tailored suits stepped into the store and looked around at various items. One stated they needed a supplier to provide large number of items on an ongoing basis. McCarthy was shown their extensive list of food needed to feed workers every Sunday. They also had a preliminary list of supplies needed for the camp when it opened next summer. The men explained how the largest Bund camp in the United States would benefit the store. However, McCarthy was uncomfortable with the request and hesitated. When pressed for an answer, McCarthy said they would have to wait and see. He agreed to think about it, and the Bund members left.[2]

McCarthy watched the Bund member's large car turning around on the dirt road. This gave Henry time to jump into his own car and follow the men up to the worksite. He was alarmed to see the number of cars parked along the old abandoned road, and large groups of people clearing the land.

Henry McCarthy knew that the first selectman needed to be informed about the camp. He immediately drove down to town leader's house, another bumpy 2-mile journey on unimproved roads.

First Selectman Ed Coer listened patiently while Henry explained everything he had seen and heard. Ed, a man of action, accompanied Henry back to the camp site where they sat in the car and observed the activity from a distance.

They counted the cars parked along the narrow roadway. In a small clearing, ladies were busy setting food out on tables. Some of the men and youths were piling brush into a large pile, while others were digging at the roots of felled trees. In the distance, the sound of an axe against tree rang through the woods.

Ed vowed that he would find the facts in the matter and take whatever action was needed. Henry knew that Ed would not let the matter rest until he had all the answers.

A group of men sat talking at the gas station on Route 6, as they did every Sunday. The rookie reporter, C. Robert "Bobby" Abbott, leaned against the building while the older men sat in the chairs they brought from home. Bobby usually was interested in the latest gossip from the local men, as he wrote short human interest articles for the *Waterbury Republican*. His goal was to be a real reporter someday. This week's news was of little interest to Bobby. He heard that Bullet Hill School was shut down this week because most of the students had chicken pox. Also, Mr. White's full flock of Thanksgiving turkeys disappeared without a trace during the night.[3] These were interesting stories, but Bobby was hoping to find out more information about the robbery the previous evening.

Bobby learned that the gas station near Lakeside Road was held up by two masked men. The seventy-year-old owner, Lou Burkhardt, was working alone when the men entered the building with their guns drawn. When they demanded money, Mr. Burkhardt pulled out his own gun and was shot during a wild exchange of bullets with the robbers. Frightened, the men ran away without the cash box. The owner was treated for a gunshot wound in his hip by Dr. Greene, who said the injury was not serious.[4]

The men's chatter paused as a black car with New York markers pulled up to the pump. While the car was being filled with gas, two of the men got out of the car. They introduced themselves as members of the German-American Bund, and they were in here in Southbury to build a recreation camp for their members. The group was looking for local men with specialized skills in cabinetry and someone to build a dam for a 5-acre swimming pond.

As the car drove off, the young reporter noticed a man in the back seat of the car, and thought he recognized the leader of the German-American Bund. Bobby raced off to tell his editor the latest news in Southbury.[5]

8
Ed Coer Takes Action

November 8, 1937, Monday

First Selectman J. Edward Coer needed to see the deed for the Bund property. Last night he talked with neighbor Basil Bass, who had been a weekend and summer resident in Southbury since 1929. His work as a corporate lawyer was based in New York City, and he had first-hand experience with the German-American Bund marching in his New York neighborhood. His recommendation to Ed was to check the deed to see who actually purchased the land. After several more suggestions, Bass promised to help Ed and Southbury in any way he could.

The more facts Ed could gather, the faster the town leaders could come up with a plan. He rushed through the morning chores around his farm on Burr Road and headed down to the town hall in South Britain.

Ed Coer had served in the town's top leadership position seven years. In addition to being a farmer and running a saw mill, Ed was on a state commission to improve rural roads. A few years previously, only the state roads through town were made of gravel or pavement while the majority of the town roads were dirt. During the winter, the unimproved roads were almost impassable for automobiles, dissolving into deep mud holes when spring arrived, but since Ed Coer was elected, his leadership to improve the local roads had made progress by using local unemployed workers funded by a grant from the state commission. Ed impressed the town with his willingness to leap into action, and making sure problems were solved.

On the way into town, Ed stopped by the Bund camp work area to check on the progress from the day before. A number of trees had been taken down and the old abandoned road was now clearly visible for a short distance. Off to the side, there was a clearing large enough to hold about twenty cars. The Bund group made a lot of progress for working just one day.

At the town hall, Ed found the town clerk, Dwight Hubbell, and his daughter, Bernice, already busy at work. They stood behind the hand-carved oak counter in front of the old safety vault. Ed asked if they had noticed any unusual property purchases recently.

Dwight reminded the first selectman that the state had been buying options on farms and houses to accumulate enough land for a training school. Also, several New Yorkers were finding peace away from the big city by building weekend and summer houses in Southbury.

Miss Hubbell retrieved the town record book from the vault and set it on the counter. She located the recent entries and showed them to Ed. On October 27, they had received a letter and deed from a Wolfgang T. Jung to list the sell in the town records. Miss Hubbell pointed out that the property was sold on September 25, a whole month before the paperwork was filed.[1]

The first selectman examined the letter and deed, noting that the deed was under the name of Wolfgang T. Jung.[2] The land was purchased by an individual. When asked why he was so interested in the property, Ed explained what he knew about the Bund building a camp in town.

Ed Coer called an emergency selectmen meeting. The other selectmen, Harry D. Platt and John J. Reynolds, were stunned when they learned of the prospect of a pro-Nazi Bund Camp in Southbury. Ed explained that he was specifically worried about the Bund's secrecy in planning the camp and delay in filing the paperwork. The selectmen were all in agreement that the Bund would need to be watched. However, at this time, they were not sure if anything could be done about it.

Even though the selectmen were not happy about the camp and were ready for a fight, they agreed with Ed to keep this information quiet. They wanted to collect the facts and decide the best course of action. If news of the camp was leaked to the public, the men decided to keep up an indifferent, professional appearance in front of the town while striving to find a legal means to stop the Bund's invasion.

Ed Coer's pursuit of a plan was not complete. His next stop was to see the town attorney, Albert Aston, for legal advice. Aston gave the several suggestions for the leader's next steps.

The first selectman had a busy week, meeting with selectmen and mayors in the area to discuss what was happening and looking for ideas. The other leaders expressed their support and encouragement.

When Ed contacted Lieutenant Schatzman of the state police, he was told there was nothing could do to stop the Bund from building their camp. The only exception was if they were doing something illegal. The state police provided Officer Olsen to help where he was needed.

By the end of the week, the FBI from Washington contacted the first selectman with ideas on how to stop the Bund from building a camp in town. They presented the example of how the residents near Camp Nordland had passed a zoning code to stop the building of additional cottages. However, since the buildings were already under construction, the zoning code did not apply to them. The code was able to prevent unwanted future construction.[3]

The FBI advised the best course of action seemed to be enacting a zoning commission. In recent experience, the Supreme Court were upholding local zoning laws against the Bund, if put into effect before any buildings were built.

Added to Southbury's advantage, the property was purchased by an individual instead of an organization or a corporation. The knowledge might give the town a little extra time to act. The other selectmen agreed with Ed that a zoning code could be their first legal avenue against the Bund camp.

Ed Coer starting to collect examples of zoning codes from other local towns. These included Roxbury, New Milford, and Waterbury. Even though he knew the town was in for a battle ahead, the first selectman finished the week with a glimmer of hope for the future.

9
The Nazis Return

November 14, 1937, Sunday

The Bund members arrived in Southbury for their second work day at Camp General von Stueben with a smaller group of workers. Only thirty-five men and boys showed up to cut down trees and to remove stumps and rocks. They were surprised to find the editor of the *Waterbury Republican* and a photographer waiting. Also with them was young reporter Bobby Abbott, who the previous week alerted the newspaper about the activities in Southbury.

The Bund members were dressed in normal clothing with no sign of a swastika or hint that they belonged to the pro-Nazi Bund. They were friendly and welcoming to the reporters. The workers willingly answered questions and posed for photographs, freely giving out their names. Today's group came from various locations in eastern New York, along with members from Stamford and Westport.

Carl Nicolay took charge of showing the reporters around the clearing and expounded on the glories of the camp they envisioned. A lodge would be placed in the meadow on top of the hill, overlooking the Pomperaug Valley. Scattered around the hillside, would be a number of cottages. Some for the staff and others for overnight visitors. There would also be hostel for the youth who were just passing through Southbury.

The children would have an area completely separate from the adults. A full 40 acres would be devoted to a camping and activity area for the youth. The highlight would be a 5-acre swimming pond made by damming a stream running through the property.

The plan was to clear enough land to begin construction in the spring. By the summer, the first group of campers would arrive. The Bund members would clear the land and construct the buildings themselves. However, there would be a few jobs for the local men with specialized skills.

The reason for the camp was the same used for Boy Scout camps and other organizational camps for years. The parents wanted to get the children away from the dirty city streets and out into the fresh air.

Carl Nicolay was affectionately called "Papa" because he was the oldest of the group. Born in Germany, Nicolay arrived in America in 1903. He proudly shared stories about being involved in the early Nazi German organizations as well as helping to organize the Bund in Chicago. Nicolay enjoyed speaking engagements every week to talk about the Bund. Just the previous evening, he was a key speaker in a gathering of German-American Bund of Bergen County, New Jersey, along with Fritz Kuhn.

Nicolay's speech that night focused on defending Adolf Hitler, claiming that Hitler was a champion of peace and a moral force of the world. He also pointed out that while America still had thousands of unemployed workers, Germany had no unemployment problem; Hitler had lifted the country out of despair and given them hope. Nicolay concluded that German-Americans should actively get involved in politics to have a voice in the American government.

Knowing that Bund Camps Andover and Siegfried had been recently in the news accused of preparing the youth for war, Nicolay told the reporters there would be no military drilling at Camp von Steuben. However, there would be a group of uniformed men on the site to who would act as guards and maintain discipline. The uniforms would be a gray shirt with the swastika on the sleeve, dark breeches, puttees on their legs, and a cap with a special insignia.

Wolfgang Jung echoed Nicolay by saying there would be no "soldiering" at the camp. Even though his name was on the property deed, it would be changed when the camp began to make a profit. At that time, the Connecticut Bund would purchase the land from him.

When asked if the German-American Bund members were Nazis, Jung stated that they were not interested what was happening in Germany. They were Americans and good citizens. Their mission was for peace and better understanding between the two nations.[1]

Bobby Abbott was excited to be on the site of the Bund camp surrounded by workers. Last Sunday he had gone to the editor to report the story of the Nazis in

Southbury. This was big news, but the editor would not publish anything until all the information was gathered and the facts were checked. The editor made a few telephone calls and confirmed the Bund was starting a camp in Connecticut. He put together a team to investigate and rewarded Bobby with an assignment. His job was to make a map of the camp's location. Bobby provided a drawing accurately depicting the town roads, the railroad and the various landmarks.

In the early afternoon, Neil Agnew, vice-president of Paramount Pictures, Inc., and his wife, actress Arlene Francis, arrived at their retreat on North George's Hill Road, near the abandoned Bullet Hill Road. Earlier in the year, the Agnews purchased two large tracts of land with a total of 90 acres. They chose this spot in a quiet part of town and well away from any activity or noise. Their newly constructed house was designed to their specifications, with plenty of room to entertain their Hollywood friends. Agnew generously provided an adjoining piece of land for his father-in-law to build a house and live nearby.[2]

The Agnews knew immediately that something had changed as they drove up to their house. The constant noise of axes and saws disturbed the peace. Agnew went to see what was happening. He was infuriated to find that the old Bullet Hill road beyond his father-in-law's house was partially cleaned of brush. A new clearing was used as a parking lot for six to eight cars.

Carl Nicolay intercepted the obviously irate gentleman took him aside to talk. After a cordial greeting, Nicolay proudly explained about the Bund and the work being done for the camp. Agnew, whose main house was in New York City, was well aware of the Bund and their anti-Semitic activities. He stomped off to tell his wife what he had learned.

Agnew decided to go down the road to see Ed Coer, and told the first selectman in no uncertain terms that Southbury needed to do something to stop the camp. With all the taxes he was paying, Agnew said he had the right to complain. The first selectman calmed him down and sent Agnew home seemingly appeased, but Agnew went directly into town to loudly voice his opinions to whoever would listen.

The Bund members prepared to leave mid-afternoon to get home before the sun set. Carl Nicolay reminded them that there would not be a work day the following Sunday.[3] They would be going to Tarrytown, New York, to place a wreath at the grave of the Carl Schurz. Schurz was a German who came to American in 1852. He became a Union General in the Civil War and a political figure. He also campaigned for Abraham Lincoln's run for the presidency. Schurz was buried in 1906.

10

Startling Revelations

November 15, 1937, Monday

Only a small of number of Southburians were aware of the German-American Bund's visits the previous two Sundays, but on this morning, the town and region learned the startling news from the *Waterbury Republican*: the largest pro-Nazi camp in America was being built in Southbury.

Not only was there a plan to build a camp in town, the work had already begun and the camp would be in operation next summer. This knowledge did not sit well with the townsfolk. Having a pro-Nazi camp in town was one thing, but learning about it for the first time from the newspaper was unsettling.

The article clearly stated the camp would hold 1,000 visitors a week with more on the weekend. With the town's population close to 1,300, the number of visitors could potentially exceed the number of residents.[1]

For many years, Southbury was able to absorb and welcome the influx of summer recreational residents, but entertaining the Nazis near the middle of town was enough to cause a panic. Worse yet, reading that thousands of Bund members would arrive on the weekends and more for special occasions was overwhelming.

The newspaper was full of information about the camp and a hand-drawn map on the front page of the paper showed its location. The camp would be in the Kettletown area, south of downtown and very near Route 6. According to the map, the train tracks ran along the length of the property. Starting near the Peter Road railroad crossing, area expanded up the hillside toward North Georges Hill Road.

At one time, Peter Road was an old wagon path to Derby. Travel along the path was used to avoid the tolls on the turnpike to Oxford and Derby, but now the narrow road was only passable for a short distance to the homes on the road. Beyond that point, the trees and brush almost obscured the old road.

The Bund planned to clear the road in the future to allow a second access to the camp and a clear way to the railroad. They could use trains to bring in visitors from New York. At both Camps Siegfried and Nordland, new railroad sidings were built to accommodate special passenger trains to stop nearby. The Bund planned to have access to the train tracks in Southbury to transport large numbers to their activities.

Since the Bund chose to start building on the top of the hill, the easiest access was from North Georges Hill Road to the old Bullet Hill Road; a route that bypassed the most populated parts of town. It appeared to some folk that the workers were sneaking into Southbury to hide their intentions.

Emotions ran high as the residents tried to figure out how the Nazi camp would affect their lives. The telephone switchboard lit up with calls to neighbors and friends, with others joining in on the party line.

After the children were sent off to school, the adults gathered in the local shops to compare notes of what they seen or heard. Many went up to the camp site to see for themselves the cleared area of the future Bund camp. They all had more questions than answers. During this time, the selectmen were uncharacteristically quiet and unavailable.

Southbury was not the only community shocked; the whole region was aghast. Editors from the major Connecticut newspapers scrambled to send their reporters to Southbury to find out what was going on. Several arrived in the same afternoon and started poking around and asking questions of anyone who would stop and talk.

The reporters soon learned that most of the townspeople knew no more than they did. Most answered with a non-committal, "no comment." The *Bridgeport Post*'s headline summed it up, "Southbury Folk Surprised, but Silent." Eventually, they did find someone who was willing to talk, but none of it could be quoted. Mr. Agnew had plenty to say, but his words were colorful and emphatic enough to "burn the ears of town officials," and not printable in the newspaper.[2]

David Roulston, the dairy farmer who gave directions to lost Bund members on their first visit, said, "They seemed nice enough." Mrs. Roulston invited the reporters into their home and served them lemonade and donuts.

The most enthusiastic response was from Lewis Dennis, a brakeman for the New Haven railroad. His family with seven children had a home near the railroad tracks and just steps away from the Bund property line. He claimed that was about time something happened in Southbury.

The first selectman's official statement gave the basic facts: The land was sold for a Nazi camp, but there is no way of regulating the landowner's use of their property. Coer did not give a personal opinion about the situation or a plan of action at this time. The newspapers reported his stance as, "If they mind their business, we'll mind ours."

Ed Coer and other town officials were attempting to handle the situation quietly and "in house."[3]

11
Not Alone

November 16, 1937, Tuesday

While the Southbury residents were trying to deal with the news of a Bund campsite on the hill, reactions were immediate in other parts of the state.

The American Legion Posts in Connecticut were among the first to denounce the Bund camp in Southbury. The parent organization, the National American Legion, in October 1937 had already stated their position against "foreign nationals conducted military training." This included the German-American Bund, the Italian Fascist League of American, and any other group that supported "an alien power or system."[1]

The Bronson-Hawley post of the American Legion in Bridgeport, Connecticut, was the first organization to go on record stating their opposition to the state's first Bund camp. A resolution that was unanimously signed by all members would be sent to other branches of the American Legion in the state, and to state officials.

The director of the Connecticut American Legion, John Reitemeyer, quickly issued a statement expressing that the swastika had no place in the state. He explained that the American Legion was against all alien doctrines in the United States, warning that the exposure of children to foreign politics would be harmful. Reitemeyer expressed a concern that was echoed by many that "Nazism and Americanism cannot exist side by side."

The Meriden American Legion, along with many others throughout the state, drafted anti-Bund resolutions and sent them to Governor Wilbur Cross.

Louis M. Altman, commander of the Stamford unit of Jewish War Veterans, gave a statement, saying that he approved of the resolution passed condemning the Southbury camp and any Nazi organization seeking to propagate their ideas in America: "These ideas and ideologies are un-American in essence, attacking the right of personal liberty, religious freedom, and creating racial hatred, and have no legitimate place in American life."

Members of the Steuben Society, a German-American organization in Hartford, immediately came under scrutiny by being compared to the Bund. Paul Stoeckel, the editor of *The Connecticut Staatzeitung*, was quick to point out the differences; he said that members of the Steuben Society were required to be American citizens, and all meetings are conducted in English. Stoeckel saw no reason to get excited about the construction of the Bund camp in Southbury.

Emil Hummel, the president of the United German-American Associations of Waterbury, had a strong opinion. He expected that the Bund would not be able to grow because there was limited immigration from Germany. Under Hitler, fewer Germans were leaving the country. Hummel observed the American-born children of German parents had no interest in the Bund's activities.

Even the Communist Committee of Connecticut made a public statement calling on Governor Wilbur L. Cross to use his power and influence to prevent the pro-Nazi camp in Southbury. I. Wofsy, the group's secretary, released the resolution that was adopted in a specially-called meeting. He called the camp an "insolent challenge to democracy."

The resolution invited all trade unions, church organizations, progressive groups, and individuals to join in this important movement to keep organized Hitlerism out of Connecticut. Southbury was surprised by the show of support from around the state. They learned they were not isolated or alone in their discomfort of having a Bund camp in their midst.

Governor Cross was astounded to receive an avalanche of letters and resolutions from all over the Connecticut about the Bund camp.[2] He decided not to take immediate action, but to wait and see how the situation played out.

12

Selectmen Call a Meeting

November 17, 1937, Wednesday, Waterbury

While the *Waterbury Republican* had been carefully fair and unbiased in their original report about the Bund, the editor of *Waterbury Republican* was ready to give his opinion. In an editorial titled "Heil Southbury!" he stated he had previously spoken out against the Nazi marching antics of the Bund camps in New Jersey and Long Island. Now he wished they had chosen a different location than Southbury, like maybe some place in Germany. While he agreed that previous immigrants had enriched the country, he worried that the current "nincompoops" stood for ideals totally opposite from America.

November 17, 1937, Wednesday, Southbury

First Selectman Ed Coer and the two other selectmen had been working quietly over the previous week to find a way to prevent the Bund from building their camp in town. Since the story was reported in the newspapers, the town was buzzing with a mixture of curiosity, anger, and fear. The newspaper reports and the anti-Bund letters in the newspaper lit a fire in the debates at every gas station, barber shop, and grocery store.

With sufficient facts in hand, the selectmen were ready to take public action. The selectmen called for a town meeting to establish a zoning commission to set up guidelines on land usage. Even though New Englanders were not keen on being told what they could do or not do, it seemed to be the best way to prevent the Bund camp from being built in town.

A warning for a special town meeting was posted at the three town message posts, at the post office, and in the grocery stores:

> Southbury, Connecticut, November 17, 1937
>
> Notice is hereby given to the legal voters of the Town of Southbury that a special Town meeting will be held in the Town Hall for the purpose of establishing a Zoning

Commission, their terms of office and to authorize the Zoning Commission to act under the provisions of Chapter 29 in the General Statutes of the State of Connecticut.

J. Edward Coer, Harry D. Platt, John Reynolds[1]

First Selectman Ed Coer made a public statement officially denying the zoning move was in any way in opposition to the Bund camp. He noted that the zoning commission was something that was needed and discussed since Route 6 officially opened through town. There were too many gas stations along the route. Besides that, chicken coops had been built in the center of town, right near the main road. The selectmen felt that zoning regulations were urgently needed to preserve the rural beauty of the town, leaving it much the same as it had been through the decades. They wanted to maintain the old New England character through town.

The notice was published in the newspapers the next day.

13
Doing Something

November 18, 1937, Thursday

Several Southbury residents decided they needed to do something to protest the German-American Bund purchasing land in town. Many met in groups to discuss options, while others wrote letters to the editors of various newspapers. One lady decided on the latter.

Known only as "a Taxpayer and a Mother in Southbury," she wrote to the *Waterbury Republican*, asking the question the whole state wanted to know. "What do the citizens of Southbury think of the pro-Nazi camp?" She firmly answered, "We do not want it."

She called for a strong leader, like Teddy Roosevelt, to emerge and drive the Nazi camps out of the United States. This unnamed mother pointed out that while Southbury children were learning about art, books, and games, the Bund was establishing military camps to teach the children to use weapons.

The taxpayer and mother called upon the mothers of Southbury to do something to stop the camp from building in Southbury. Her recommendation was for the mothers to take action, and to not to depend on the town officials. However, she did not offer any suggestions on how the mothers would stop the camp. She ended her letter by saying "Wake up New England!"[1]

In Kettletown, the residents near the Bund property had a small meeting. They chose to protest by educating the residents of Southbury about the Bund and *Bundesführer* Fritz Kuhn's plot to build an army to conquer America.

Basil Bass recommended sharing the *American* magazine's five-page article titled "An American Fuhrer Organizes An Army," by Joseph Dinneen. He secured enough reprints to distribute to all of the Southbury households. The group decided to write a cover letter in bold, block printing:

> Every Citizen and Resident of Southbury—ATTENTION
> The attached article describes an organization which purposes to overrun YOUR town. Please read it and then decide whether or not you want the swastika and goose step thrust upon you, whether you want your land values depressed. If you do not want these things, which the German-American Bund carries with it everywhere, attend the Town Meeting next Tuesday afternoon and do your civic duty.
>
> The Kettletowners[2]

The envelopes were stuffed with the letter and article, and addressed by Basil Bass's staff. The packets were mailed to each Southbury household from New York City, with the expected delivery on Saturday.

In the White Oak section of Southbury, closest to the Woodbury border, a gas station owner decided he had to do something. George Holmes, a dogmatic patriot, had taken over the business from his uncle several years previously. His gas station also had a small convenience store with candy, basic groceries, and a large selection of newspapers and magazines.

During the world war, Holmes worked in New Haven for the Winchester Repeating Arms Company. Afterwards, he was a master mechanic for the Uniroyal Rubber Company in Naugatuck. While not considering himself an activist, he was often involved in local causes. He was a previous commander of the Sons of Union Veterans.

George Holmes wrote to the editor of the *Waterbury Republican* saying that the Nazi camp in Southbury was a matter of grave concern for everyone in America. He quoted Joseph Dinneen's article in the *Reader's Digest*, which proclaimed the American Nazis were a threat to democracy. Holmes warned that the camps were a training ground for the Nazis to infiltrate their philosophies into the American culture.

Holmes gave a call to action that ended in a warning; he compelled the readers write to their legislators and demand that laws be provided and enforced to stop Nazi activities in Connecticut. He added, "Tomorrow may be too late."[3]

The *Waterbury Republican* was well aware at all the Bund press coverage around the state. In the day's editorial, "Queer Friendship Tactics," the editor spoke out about the Bund's tactics. He pointed out if the Bund wanted to make friends in Connecticut, they were going about it the wrong way. They were building a camp in Southbury while claiming there would be no military or soldier action. However, it had been well-reported the camps in New Jersey and Long Island appeared to have military action and through flying a flag of a foreign power and wearing foreign military uniforms.[4]

14

Reverend Lindsay Writes a Letter

November 18, 1937, Thursday

Reverend M. E. N. Lindsay paced anxiously around his office. The town was filled with turmoil since the news of the Bund camp in Kettletown. Few people knew what to think or how they should feel about the camp. It did not help that the selectmen were not discussing the situation publicly. Their lack of open sharing created a void for leadership.

On several occasions while attending Yale, Rev. Lindsay had the opportunity to warn against the dangers of the Nazis, and did so. Not saying anything to his congregation would be wrong. He felt an obligation to confront the matter head on.

Lindsay called Rev. Felix Manley of the Federated Church to compare their ideas. Manley had also been keeping up with the Nazi's systematic persecution of the pastors and priests in Germany. The Protestant and Catholic churches were being closed by law, and a new Nazi religion was organized and pushed upon the country.

Rev. Manley graduated from Yale Divinity School in 1935, and then worked for the New Haven Council of Churches for a couple of years. He became the pastor in Southbury barely six months ago. Manley agreed with Lindsay that they needed to take action. They decided that a display of strong spiritual leadership was needed. Both pastors would use a part of their Sunday sermon to state their case: the pro-Nazi Bund camp would be dangerous to Southbury.

In the meantime, Lindsay knew what to do. Pulling out his typewriter, he started writing letters.[1] Rev. Lindsay's first letter was addressed to the editor of the *Waterbury Republican*. He congratulating the paper's stand regarding the camp in Southbury. The paper was an active and fearless ally in the cause of Christian principles. Lindsay expressed his alarm at the insidious Nazi movement, which he considered the Anti-Christ. Lindsay wrote: "I am compelled to warn our people of the evil consequences of such movements." He added that he would be addressing the issue in his sermon on Sunday.

In a letter to *The Advance*, a Christian magazine for Congregational churches, Lindsay got right to the point. His letter stated: "May I bring to your attention the move to establish a Pro-Nazi camp in the town of Southbury." After he gave an overview of the camp, he reported there was "much resentment within the Township" over this proposal. Lindsay strongly stated: "I want to do what I can to register the opposition of the church to this alien and Un-Christian movement."

The message to the *Christian Century*, a nation-wide Christian magazine, was similar to the previous one. Lindsay wanted it on the record that he would publically oppose the pro-Nazi movement. With the fact that the Nazis had come to Southbury, he was doubly determined to spread the warning across the nation. Lindsay offered to send a copy of his sermon to be published in the magazine.

With the spiritual side covered, Rev. Lindsay was ready to turn to the government. In his letter to the Governor Wilbur Cross, he explained the Bund's plans in Southbury, then proceeded to say, "I need to remind you that the principles of the said body are entirely Un-American. They are a denial of the very Democracy they use to establish their camp." The freedom of speech in America allowed the Bund to say and stand for the principles of Hitler, who was absolutely against the same freedom. Lindsay strongly urged the governor to take action by assigning the attorney-general to investigate. "And if it be legally possible, to put a stop to the spread of this movement."

Writing to his congressman in Washington, D.C., Rev. Lindsay told J. Joseph Smith, "We oppose this movement not only within Southbury, but within the United States." Lindsay asked if there was legal way to stop the Bund, and if not, one should be made. He pressed his case, saying that even if Nazism was permitted within a Democracy, an overt act was committed when a semi-military camp was established to spread this view. Lindsay urged Congressman Smith to use his position to "bring about a corrective measure."

Reverend Lindsay sat back and looked at the pile of letters. This was all he could do right now, but the fight had only just begun.

15
Bund Marches in New Haven

November 20, 1937, Saturday

On Saturday evening, the German-American Bund held a large meeting in the Convention Hall of New Haven. It was a massive display of uniformed *Ordnungsdienst* (O.D.), the group's elite security guards. They marched with banners of their various units from the New York groups of South Brooklyn, Jamaica, Bronx, New York, White Plains, New Rochelle, and Yonkers. The Bund was showing the force of their organization as they were trying to start a Bund unit in New Haven. The *New Haven Register* published a photograph of the marchers, along with the audience saluting in the Nazi manner.

Key speakers of the evening were Bund leaders Wilhelm Boehning and Carl Nicolay. They explained the aims and purposes of the Bund, and gave updates on the latest Youth Camps. This included a report on Camp General von Stueben and discussions on how to increase Bund membership in the area. In response to the many newspaper articles and resolutions against the Bund, Nicolay said, "It is wrong to call us Nazis." He explained that the Bund was fighting for America "first, last and all the time."[1]

Wilhelm Boehning spoke on the growing issue of Bund meetings being disturbed by protestors. He recommended that the O.D. needed to be expanded. He said, "O.D. is a growing necessity in our struggle and is at the heart of our movement today." His comment brought a large positive response from the audience. The group voted to begin an *Ordnungsdienst* group in New Haven and appointed Paul Schlenther as its leader.[2]

The visiting groups spent the night in New Haven before heading to New York the next day.

16
War of Words

November 21, 1937, Sunday

Those searching the Sunday papers for new information about the Bund in Southbury were not disappointed. *The New York Times* Sunday magazine featured a four-page spread titled "Hitler enlists the German Everywhere," by Otto D. Tolischus. The startling article revealed that anyone with German heritage within the last four generations automatically fell under Nazi law. No matter where this person lived in the world, they were part of a German community of blood and destiny. Their birthright obligated them to surrender to a new loyalty and new discipline supplied under Adolf Hitler's control.[1]

People's reaction to the news was varied. Overall, the article appeared to add millions of people to the Nazi grand list. If all of the people whose great, great, grandparents were of German blood stood with Hitler, then the Nazis could easily conquer the world.

Carl Nicolay's Letter to the Editor

The *Waterbury Republican* continued their coverage about the Bund camp in Southbury. On this Sunday morning, there was a letter to the editor from Carl Nicolay, the eastern divisional organizer of the German-American Bund. Nicolay had served as a gracious host to the editor, a reporter, and photographer the previous week at the campsite, proudly showing off the land and explaining the future activities of the camp. The editor of the newspaper sent a copy to the headquarters of the German-American Bund in New York City. The Bund officials were happy with the article.

Carl Nicolay wrote a long response complimenting the *Republican* on its fairness in dealing with the subject of the Bund and the campsite. In his experience, not many editors treated the Bund with fair reporting. He did, however, dispute the claim from David Roulston who stated that the Bund camp would lower the value of his land.

Nicolay's comparison with the Long Island camps was heart-stopping for the Southbury readers. He said at Camp Siegfried, the town went from being dead to humming with new people and business. He explained that the German-Americans bought many plots of the land throughout the village and became permanent residents. Yaphank, previously a town of 2,000 people, quickly grew with the additional Bund members, and even though there was a real estate boom, and new businesses were built, the village lost its small town atmosphere to become a place where thousands of pro-Nazis gathered during the summer.

Camp Nordland in New Jersey was another successful real estate venture. The Bund brought to the town of Andover good will and increased business, according to Nicolay. He claimed that David Roulston and others in Kettletown would not only be able to sell their land, but the land values would increase in the entire area. Bund members from all over the area would want to come live in Southbury, near the new camp. Nicolay tried to quiet the fears of Southbury residents by portraying himself as fair-minded, open, and honest.

Nicolay was quick to remind the editor that the German-American Bund was an American group with a goal to build understanding and friendship. He should have stopped right there, but continued by saying, "based on the principles and ideals of Adolf Hitler." Carl Nicolay said that someday Americans would appreciate the German-American Bund because they were ready and prepared to stand by "flag and country, Constitution and rightful government." While the letter had a friendly tone, filled with understanding, there were statements that caused un-ease among the Southbury residents. If Nicolay's goal was to set aside the fears of the town, he went about it the wrong way. Did he really think the town wanted to be like Yaphank, New York, and have hundreds of Bund members living in their midst? Even though the Bund leadership carefully said they were not in any way connected with the Nazi regime in Germany, Nicolay claimed directly that they followed the Nazi leader, Adolf Hitler.[2]

George Holmes' Letter to the Editor

In contrast to Carl Nicolay's letter to the editor, George Holmes' letter was a dogmatic, strongly worded tirade against the Bund. In a letter under the heading of "George Holmes Claims Bund is Illegal Group," Holmes declared the Bund camp was an invasion and a conspiracy.

In Holmes' viewpoint, there was no doubt that the arrival of the Bund in Southbury was an invasion. According to the dictionary, an invasion is described as "the incoming or first attack of anything hurtful or pernicious." Based on information in the recent *Reader's Digest*'s article claiming the Bund had an army and planned to take over the world, Holmes concluded that Southbury was definitely in danger. Holmes said he had papers and articles providing proof Kuhn reported directly to Hitler. Therefore, Hitler was ultimately behind the Southbury invasion.

Holmes said the conspiracy was stated in the Bund's purpose for the youth camps: "...to regenerate America by use of these youths under our direction." Their plan was clearly to train the youth as Hitler's future military force to be used against America. Holmes called for the governor to act quickly to call on the federal government to help get rid of the Bund in Southbury.[3]

17
The Pastors Speak Out

November 21, 1937, Sunday

On a normal Sunday morning before Thanksgiving, parishioners would expect to hear a sermon about being thankful, especially during hard times. Both Rev. Lindsay and Rev. Manley had decided the situation called for a different focus.

Reverend Lindsay looked out over at his congregation. The normal members were in their favorite seats, while his three little girls sat in the front row.[1] He had wondered if his letter to the editor would bring any visitors to hear today's unusual sermon.

In the overview of the five-points he planned to cover, the congregation learned there was no chance they would hear a sweet Thanksgiving talk, especially not when the key words were anti-Christ, Nazis, and insidious menace.

Lindsay started with a basic definition for an anti-Christ as any person or persons whose principles, policies or practices that deny the historical Christ. The Nazi's new religion was similar to Christianity, but it added pagan mythology with Teutonic legions. This led to the Aryan cult and lie of a superior German race. In doing so, they excluded the validity of the historical Christ. Not only does it deny Christ, it persecutes the Church, seeking to destroy the guiding principles. Therefore, the Nazis are anti-Christ.

The evidence to prove the Bund was controlled by the Nazi government was simple. Carl Nicolay, the Bund's eastern organizer and visitor to Southbury had recently spent a year in Germany, lecturing about the glories of the Bund's activities in America. If the Nazis did not support the Bund and their camps, then Nicolay would not have been welcomed there. He must have shown the camps were favorable to the Nazi views.

A pattern emerged, based on the history of the other Bund camps. The German heritage children were enticed to attend the camps with the offer of exciting programs. Even though the only language spoken was German, the children enjoyed the comradery of the group and were unaware that the songs they sang were full of hateful meaning. The activities included marching and drilling in a militaristic manner. Several of the camps included barracks for Stormtroopers.

If a camp was allowed to come to Southbury unchallenged, what would this be the future of this camp? Or the future of Southbury? Lindsay concluded that the Bund camps were un-Christian, un-American as they follow the philosophy of a foreign government, and pro-Nazi by the admission of its own leaders.

Rev. Lindsay's recommendation for action was to deport any alien connected to the Bund. Also, any naturalized citizen who supported the Bund would be violating their oath to America because they practiced the views of a foreign government. Anyone who defied their oath should lose their American citizenship.

Lindsay's most attainable suggestion was to write the local representatives in Congress and to the Connecticut governor, Wilbur Cross. The next suggestion in the sermon notes was scribbled out, but it said, "Locally, pass a zoning regulation, which may result in refusing permission to build, if such a building would prove undesirable to the community as a whole." Whether or not Lindsay decided to share that comment is unknown.

Rev. Lindsay closed his sermon with, "Let us therefore take council together my friends, and lend our efforts to the cause of the Righteousness of Christ, beginning with our community, and extending to the uttermost parts of the earth."[2]

On the opposite side of town, Reverend Felix Manley's sermon devoted only a portion to the subject of the Bund. He began with a reference in the Psalm 23, which says, "my cup runneth over," in a sermon titled "Thanksgiving for Thanksliving." While it is easy to say the words "thank you," it is hard to live "thank you" by being appreciative for what we have and the people around us. But we should especially give thanks for our rich heritage, for the America, the land we love.

Manley felt that democracy itself was in danger, as fascism and communism were ideals trying to take over the world. Both were opposite of the Christian principles of love, liberty and "loyalty to God." Southbury realized how fragile freedom can be with the proposed pro-Nazi camp coming to town. It is okay if the Germans wanted to create a place to gather for picnics and recreation. The problem is the ideologies of the Nazi government would extend into the community. Especially the statement a German national would always be a part of Germany, and therefore, under the rule of Hitler.

> This camp is obviously planned as a training station for young Hitler youth who will stretch their arms in the Nazi salute and "Heil Hitler" with all that it implies. America is a melting pot for all of those who desire to the Americans. It is not a picnic ground in which un-American inhabitants can tear down what has been built so slowly and at so much cost.

Rev. Manley continued. The fascist and communist are filling their children with hateful principles: of atheism, paganism and materialism. Are American children learning the value their citizenship and the responsibilities that come with it? Do they know what a privilege free speech is and to be able to vote for their government?

"If democracy is to endure, we must rekindle the flame which now seems to be burning low. We must prepare the world for the children of tomorrow."[3]

Russell H. Warner, leader of the Everyman's Bible class at the St. Paul's Methodist Church in South Britain also had a few things to say about the Bund camp in Southbury. He claimed the Bund was trying to walk on a narrow line between the American flag and the Swastika. However, Warner claimed most of Southbury believed whoever raises their hand in salute of a foreign dictator is obviously trying to straddle both sides.

Warner's questions were thought provoking. Will the Bund need permission from Hitler to have picnics in Southbury? To show we support free speech, must we fly swastika flags around town to prove it?

Warner pointed out the Bund members are supposed to have their American citizenship papers, and agree to preserve the fundamentals of democracy. By doing so, is making the assumption their loyalty is to America. But the papers alone give no guarantee of patriotism. Warner reminded the men we cannot judge a person's heart, but we can judge them by their previous and future actions. "No man can be loyal to the ideals of Hitler and remain a good American citizen."[4]

Rabbi Abraham J. Feldman, rabbi of Temple Beth Israel of West Hartford, and creator of the *Jewish Ledger* newspaper, spoke out against the Bund camp. His recommendation was to make the Bund feel "as unwelcome as possible"[5]in Connecticut. He said the Bund was "subversive of everything that is nobly and decently American."[6]

In Feldman's Thanksgiving sermon, he praised Southbury for doing everything they could to prevent the establishment of the pro-Nazi camp. He said most Americans choose to preserve the American ideal where "freedom is not assassinated, the dignity of man is glorified and peace is the coveted ideal of national policy." Feldman continued, "It is such Americans that have given the stirring demonstration of devotion in unpolluted Americanism in Southbury yesterday."[7]

The Ministers Association of Waterbury was slow to express an opinion about the situation in Southbury. They were involved with hearings about low-income housing, however, the keynote speaker did not appear because of illness. Even though it was not on the agenda, the ministers talked about the Bund and whether they should put out a statement. They could not come to a conclusion on what to say, and decided to table it for another month. The *Waterbury Democrat* titled their article about the meeting as "Ministers' Association Splits On Discussion Of Bund Camp." By the time the next meeting was scheduled, it appeared that the Bund was no longer a threat in Connecticut.

18
Special Town Meeting

November 23, 1937, Tuesday

The day of the special town meeting finally arrived. The town leaders declared a half-holiday and the shops and business closed at noon. All six one-room schoolhouses finished early to allow time for the children to arrive home before the meeting, giving the adults one less thing to worry about, but according to the newspapers, there was plenty to worry about.

The papers were full of conflicting information and opinions. One unnamed town official said he expected confrontations about the Bund camp at the special meeting. He stated the town was too agitated and needed a forum for discussion, and he expected the meeting would develop into a protest meeting.

Some people feared that uniformed Nazis would come out in force to defend their right to build the campsite. While others speculated the Bund members would goose-step down the street preventing the meeting-goers access to the town hall, but none of that happened; in fact, there was not a foreign uniform in sight.[1]

A few old-timers arrived at the town hall early to stake out the warmest seats near the potbelly stove. Dozens of chairs were crammed together filling up all available space in the small room. The town hall was built in 1873 to hold the town offices and records, and to hold meetings. Residents pushed in until there was no room, leaving the last arrivals spilling out the door and onto the road.

Promptly at 2 o'clock, First Selectman J. Edward Coer called the meeting to order.[2] Noting the large crowd, Rev. M.E.N. Lindsay offered the use of his church a short distance down the road. Upon a quick agreement, the meeting was adjourned, with the admonition that everyone needed to be in church by 2:20 sharp. Rev. Lindsay ran ahead to start the coal furnace in the basement of the church.

Newspaper photographers who had been standing outside the town hall, scattered around trying to capture images of the various town characters walking toward the church. They documented the variety of people who called Southbury home, including the farmers in overalls and men in hunting jackets. Others were in casual clothes while some wore their Sunday best, and the rich summer residents were splendidly decked out in their warm fur coats.

The first selectman from Woodbury was spotted among the group, along with officials from other towns who were interested in the zoning process. The whole board of selectmen from New Milford attended along with businessmen from Waterbury, Torrington, and other towns. As the crowd walked down the center of the street, they avoided the vehicles of various sizes parked along the side.

Ahead stood the white church with a tall white spire reaching into the blue sky illuminated by the fall sunshine. Before the town hall was built, the church was also used for town meetings. Inside the cold church, people quickly filled the pews on the main floor and spread up into the balcony. Newspaper photographers staked out places where they could see the most action. Once the pews were filled, the rest of the people stood along the walls, three or four deep.

Several school children were among the audience, sitting with their parents.[3] A couple of infants cooed and fussed in their mother's arms. One baby hiccupped loudly; the sound echoing through the old structure. A wave of friendly chuckles spread across the room. Irishman Gregory Cassidy, Democratic town chairman, turned around in his seat near the front and smiled broadly at the infant.

First Selectman Coer reconvened the special town meeting exactly on time. Rev. Lindsay was elected as the meeting chairman, a position he had served previously. He was known to run a meeting in a calm and fair manner.

The official notice of special meeting was read by Assistant Town Clerk Miss Bernice Hubbell, underlining its purpose was for "establishing a Zoning Commission, their terms of office and to authorize the Zoning Commission to act."[4]

When Lindsay entered the sanctuary after stoking the fire, he learned that he had been selected as the meeting chairman. Accepting the position graciously, he reminded the crowd that anyone who was a legal voter or property owner had the right to speak in a town meeting. Lindsay admonished the group that the only discussion allowed would be about the zoning commission.

Knowing that the people wanted to discuss the Bund camp, Rev. Lindsay stated no mention of "that other matter" would be allowed at the official town meeting. However, he offered the use of the church for a second meeting, saying, "Anyone wanting to talk about it are welcome to stay here as long they want."

First Selectman Coer explained a zoning commission job was to write the zoning ordinances for the town and implement them. Their goal would be to keep the majority of the community as residential and farming districts, along with industrial and business area. They would also designate areas for recreational purposes and summer developments.

Immediately, Gregory Cassidy jumped to his feet and said, "I move that Southbury be not zoned." Herbert H. Sears seconded the motion. The startled first selectman explained that the motion was not stated in the proper wording to match the called purpose. Mr. Cassidy made several attempts at finding the right words and made a new motion, stating, "That the town of Southbury does not establish a Zoning Commission." A vote was taken with twenty-one voters approving. The "no" votes were not counted because there was such a large number of hands raised. Cassidy's motion was soundly defeated. Mr. Coer reread the official motion which was quickly seconded by George Holmes.

A lively debate erupted among the townspeople, wondering how the zoning code would affect them. The photographers moved around the room to get pictures of the speakers, and reactions from the people. Mary Hickok voiced the concerns of the farmers who were worried about their land and livelihood. She, and many of the farmer's wives, ran farm stands. They were told that the stands could still operate along Route 6.

Mr. Coer carefully reassured everyone that the zoning commission would try to preserve the atmosphere of the town, but there were "too many gas stations and chicken coops along the Country Road," the current Main Street. He also said that there would be careful consideration of all residents and their needs.

The town's attorney, Albert Aston, gave a report on the surrounding towns and their discussions to adopt zoning regulations. He stated that the zoning idea was "not entirely instigated by a recent development." In fact, he said, "As far back as 1930 a group residents of this town organized a committee to consider a zoning code." Mr. Aston explained that the code could be appealed, as provided by law, in case the zoning became a burden.

One photographer was determined to get a photograph of Ed Coer, who was continually pacing around the room. Every time the photographer set up his shot, Coer would pivot and walk away. Several people became aware of this game, as other impassioned residents stated their opinion about zoning. The photographer became more determined, changing his position several times to catch the First Selectman unawares.

Mr. Lloyd Faller asked for specific details about the plans of the zoning commission. However, no details could be given because the commission was not yet established. Thinking he was just receiving a run around, Faller was mildly disgusted and sat down saying, "All right, you refuse."

Still stalking Coer, the photographer hid behind a column and jumped out in front of him causing the flash bulb to light up directly into the first selectman's face. Dazed, Ed Coer retreated to a corner, while the photographer smiled smugly.

Asking to be heard, the dairy farmers requested that the meeting be kept short because they needed to leave by 3 p.m. to go take care of their animals. The discussion time was closed, and the vote was called to establish a zoning commission. By the raising of hands, the motion was passed with 122 people voting yes and forty-one voting no.

Rev. Lindsay made a motion to appoint a nominating committee. The three selectmen were immediately chosen to select five men to serve on the new zoning commission. J. Edward Coer, Harry D. Platt and John J. Reynolds took a moment for short private discussion.

Miss Jennie Hinman stood up saying she wished to make a resolution concerning the American flag. Miss Hinman was a matronly and imposing woman, whose relatives were the earliest settlers of Southbury. She was a popular socialite who resided in New York City, and had summered in Southbury all her life. Miss Hinman had recently moved to Southbury full time.

When Rev. Lindsay gently reminded Miss Hinman the subject was out of order in the current meeting, she indignantly said, "I don't think that anything in regard to the American flag would be out of order in this meeting." With the promise that the subject could be addressed at the meeting to follow, Miss Hinman took her seat.

The nominating committee was ready to choose the zoning commission with their list of prospects. The process went quickly, because the potential commissioners were asked ahead of time about their willingness to serve. The nominees included a diverse group of men: Attorney Albert Aston; Leslie Wheeler, a building contractor; Henry McCarthy, a retail merchant; Herbert Wells, real estate salesman; and Robert C. Mitchell, finance board chairman. No one openly disagreed with the choice of commissioners, and the men were approved.[5]

With the main business completed, the dairy farmers started to make their move toward the door. First Selectman Coer quickly concluded the meeting saying, "Voting for a zoning commission today is just the first step. There is no limit to what can be done together." The special town meeting was adjourned.

The three selectmen followed the farmers out, saying they did not want a public opinion meeting to be confused with the official town meeting. The second meeting had nothing to do with town policies.

A number of the attendees left the building after the special town meeting ended. Many had to get home to families, animals, businesses, or felt that the goal of the day had been reached. Several of the newspapermen who had been in the balcony, came down to sit among the townspeople. Others walked outside to try to get a few interviews before they sent their story out into the world.

One reporter caught up with the first selectmen on the steps of the church. Coer was obviously unhappy at the amount of attention the town was getting in the newspapers. "The matter has been stirred up by the press," Mr. Coer declared. "Southbury can cope with whatever situation may arise from Nazi activities at the Bund camp when, and if, such matters become cause for public concern."

Coer continued by saying that the newspapers had been publishing the opinions of a group chosen by themselves as mouthpieces to speak for Southbury. He stated that this was creating friction between neighbors, and brought sensation-seekers to Southbury from every part of Connecticut and New York.

19
Mass Indignation

November 23, 193, Tuesday Afternoon

Before the church building was even cleared, George Holmes, in a surprise move, jumped up onto the platform and stated, "History may be in the making in this little church today and it rests with us as to whether that history shall have an honored place in the annals of our country or be remembered as only an empty gesture."

Rev. M. E. N. Lindsay interrupted and suggested that a meeting chairman should be selected. The pastor was once again chosen to moderate the public meeting. He explained this meeting was not official, unlike the town meeting which followed the rules of order. Lindsay said, "I have no authority over you and must ask your indulgence and good sportsmanship in the conduct of this meeting. Everyone is allowed to speak, no matter where they are from."

A number of people started speaking at once. Lindsay recommended that each person raise their hand to be recognized to speak. The restrained emotions of the people was evident. Various speakers expressed their fears and worries about the situation. A few gave colorful speeches, and Lindsay had to remind a few they were inside a church with women and children.

The rich and celebrity land-owners of Kettletown were out in full force. Many were concerned about their land values being reduced with the Bund camp nearby. Attorney Basil Bass spoke against the Bund, sharing his first-hand experiences at his main home in New York City. He stated, "If you don't keep them out, we'll sell out and move away here." As several people nodded, he indicated that he was speaking for the other New York summer residents also.

The floor was finally turned over to George Holmes, who ran a gas station and snack shop in the White Oak district of town. Since the announcement of the Bund camp, Holmes had written strongly worded letters to the editors of the *Waterbury Republican* opposing the German-American Bund camp. In the tone of a fire and brimstone preacher, Holmes said:

> Mr Chairman. That which is taking place in our midst, and which is the primary cause of this assemblage today, is of too grave an import to be lightly considered and dismissed with this local meeting. The object of our concern is nation-wide, yes, world-wide, in its scope. The very foundation of our national security is being undermined by treasonable agents of an alien government hiding behind the guise of American citizens.

The audience was mesmerized by this unexpected, passionate speaker, and leaned forward, devoting their full attention to Holmes.

Holmes, aware that a portion of Southbury residents were of German descent, made sure his point was clear. "We have nothing against the old order German, it is the New Germans we have a problem with." The New Germans were the ones aligned with Adolf Hitler and the Nazi regime. "Their plan to Nazi-ize America is obvious. Their principles deny the sanctity of home. It is up to us to preserve America for Americans. Let us bring pressure for the enactment of national legislation, for if we remain idly by, we will be ruined."

Holmes read a resolution he had written.[1] He hoped the people would accept it and sign copies of it. Holmes said the original copy would be sent to the president, with copies sent to the governor, Senate, and Congress.

The resolution, in seven short paragraphs, stated that the people of Southbury were aware that a parcel of land in the town had been purchased for a recreation camp for Nazi-American youths. The purpose of the camp was to teach the youths the philosophy of Nazis, with the expressed purpose of dominating national affairs. The Bund's goals were "unfriendly acts of conspiracy and invasion of the town."

At the end of the empowered reading of the resolution, the audience exploded in applause. A motion was made to accept it, but before Robert's Rules of Order transpired to complete the motion, Miss Jennie Hinman stood up to say that she had a resolution, "that only the American flag could fly in Southbury." There was an immediate outcry from members of the Veterans of Foreign Wars, who explained that the flags of our allies should be allowed to fly alongside the American flag.

After several attempts to form an acceptable resolution, Miss Hinman became flustered. A reporter from the *Hartford Courant* offered to help and sat next to her in the pew while they worked together on the exact working of the resolution.

Rev. Lindsay steered the meeting back to the Holmes resolution for a voice vote, which was accepted without a single "nay." George Holmes said, "We need to beware of citizens of alien governments hiding behind the guise of American citizens."

Rev. Lindsay turned the meeting's attention back to Miss Hinman to see if her resolution was ready. On her behalf, the reporter stood on the platform and read the revised flag resolution: "Be it resolved that the display of any emblem or any flag not accompanied by the American flag, on any land or water in this township, or the wearing of any dress of uniform indicating allegiance to any foreign power on public roads or streams in this community shall be prohibited and forbidden." The resolution passed, and everyone looked expectantly at the chairman.

Looking around the room, Lindsay asked if anyone else had something to say; there was no answer. Seeing many unfamiliar faces among the audience, he then asked, "Is there any representative of the German-American Bund here who wants to be heard?" Again, no answer.

Miss Hinman rose, and suggested the singing of the "Star-Spangled Banner" to close the meeting. Rev. Lindsay agreed, but asked permission to first offer a prayer. Lindsay prayed, calling to God for guidance "As we see these things that are un-Christian, may we do what we can in a Christian way to abolish them. May we do so in the spirit of the loving Christ, because we desire to save all mankind rather than condemn it, and are not against men, but against movement that hurt men." A moment of silence followed before Rev. Lindsay said, "Amen."

Seated at the piano, Henry Cunningham began the introduction to the national anthem. With James Wilson leading the singing, the community of voices rose dramatically as one, and the music soared to the climax of the song. Photographers pointed their cameras toward the ceiling. As the "rockets red glare, the bombs bursting in air" was sung, the flash bulbs created pops and flashes adding to the emotion of the moment. As the last note ended, a silence settled around the room, and a moment of complete calm reigned.

Before anyone could move from their seat, George Holmes broke the silence reminding everyone to come forward and sign the resolution. Rev. Lindsay admonished the reporters with a smile to not walk off with any of the copies of the resolution. Many people went forward to sign the document that day, and more copies were distributed around the town for additional signatures.

Democrat leader Gregory Cassidy walked out of the meeting shaking his head, disturbed by the mostly Republican zoning commission and the emotional outbursts he had heard. "It's all a racket," he said. "That's all it is."

Washington, D.C.

Unknown to the citizens of Southbury, exactly at the same time as the special town meeting was held, the U.S. Congress were discussing the proposed Nazi camp at Southbury on the floor of the House of Representatives in Washington, D.C. Representative Samuel Dickstein of New York, told the house that unless action was taken, "thousands of Nazis will soon be goose-stepping in Connecticut."

20
Fritz Kuhn's Bad Day

November 24, 1937, Wednesday, Bund Headquarters, NYC

Fritz Kuhn, leader of the German-American Bund, was not having a good day. The newspapers were full of anti-Bund articles.

The news of Southbury's town meeting made headlines across the country, accompanied by a photograph of the crowds entering the Congregational Church.

All eyes were turned toward the little town trying to keep the Nazis from invading. The explosion of national publicity was a shock to everyone, including the Bund. The nation waited anxiously to see how the Bund would respond to the village that dared to prevent the Nazis from building a recreation camp.

The press contacted Carl Nicolay directly at his home in New York City for a statement. He told the *Hartford Courant* that he would not comment until he had talked with "the observers we had at the meeting." He claimed the Bund had placed spies in Southbury, and he had not received their report. "They were ordered to simply watch peacefully, and not engage in any arguments with the residents." When pressed for additional comment or a reaction from Fritz Kuhn, Nicolay promised there would be an answer, "probably next week."

Without the expected explosive reaction from the Bund leaders, the newspapers came to their own conclusions. The *Hartford Courant*'s headline blasted, "Bund's Camp In Southbury Seen Doomed," claiming that the plans for the camp were virtually dead. Other newspapers declared that Southbury had won their battle. A Waterbury editorial said that Hitler's followers should realize by now they are not welcomed in Connecticut. "They are moving into hostile territory and though ecstatic heils may echo in the camp proper, there will be the dour Yankee equivalent of the Bronx cheer in the territory around about."

In truth, the Bund leadership at this moment was less worried about Southbury because they were occupied with bigger problems.

Bund Headquarters, New York City

Closer to home, Kuhn was especially infuriated with Judge J. Wallace Leyden of New Jersey. Leyden served as naturalization judge and administered the U.S. citizenship oath to immigrants. On November 19, the judge told a group of German applicants, "You can't be both an American and a German. You must be either one of the other. I consider membership in the German-American Bund sufficient grounds for denying citizenship." The judge continued saying that immigrants must make a choice, especially coming from a country run by a dictator; either for America of the other country.[1]

Fritz Kuhn was immediately on the defensive, denying that Hitler was a dictator. Kuhn lashed out at Judge Leyden calling him names and threatening him, telling him to change his views. For extra measure, Kuhn wrote letters protesting Leyden's statement to the State Department and the Department of Justice. He tried to gather enough support to impeach the judge. Kuhn even filed a law suit against him.

At the same time, the little village of Southbury was receiving national attention with their antagonism against building Camp General von Steuben. The local pastors had preached scathing anti-Bund sermons, the neighbors near the camp had distributed an article that made the Bund look like they were trying to take over

America. To top it off, Southbury's well-publicized town meeting was causing a stir across the country. Something needed to be done.[2]

Kuhn decided a Bund presence was required in Southbury. They needed to show Southbury they would not back down because of one town meeting. Fritz Kuhn decided that this would be a good job for Gerhard "Wilhelm" Kunze.

Wilhelm Kunze was a first generation American, born in Philadelphia. His German parents made sure he was integrated into the American lifestyle, but during the world war, young Kunze was ridiculed at school because of his German name. Even though Kunze was a young man, he was already the president of the Philadelphia branch of the Bund. His fervor for the Bund's aims and purposes got him noticed by Kuhn.

William Kunze assisted with the organization and opening of the youth camp, Camp Nordland, in Andover, New Jersey. He spoke at the dedication ceremony on July 18, 1937, alongside the Bund fuhrer. Kuhn was so impressed he was sent young Kunze to Stuttgart, Germany, as the Bund representative. Kunze would be one of the speakers as a presiding officer of the Fifth Reich Congress of Foreign Germans.

Dressed in his Bund uniform, Kunze gave one of the principal speeches. He praised the aims and achievements of the Third Reich, and condemned the Jews and their influence in the United States. When he returned to America by ship, he was met at the dock by Fritz Kuhn and a following of reporters.[3]

At a Bund rally a week later, on November 16, Kuhn announced Kunze was a new member of his staff in New York City, with the position of "National Propaganda Leader." The title was quickly changed to "National Publicity Leader," which was more agreeable to Americans.

Kuhn decided that Kunze was the right person to present the Bund's case and calm the fears of the small Connecticut town. The Bund staff made the arrangements for Kunze to visit Southbury and scheduled meetings with Reverend Lindsay and Reverend Manley individually. Each pastor would have two hours of one-on-one conversation and gentle persuasion. With Thanksgiving the next day, Sunday afternoon was chosen as the meeting date.

When Kunze was finished talking with the pastors, he planned to check on the progress at Camp General von Steuben and encourage the workers. Fritz Kuhn made it clear to Kunze he expected no additional problems from the small town of Southbury.

Southbury

Reverends Lindsay and Manley met together ahead of the meeting and decided to listen to Wilhelm Kunze with an open mind, without expressing any arguments. Afterward, each would write a summary letter to Kunze to make sure they understood the Bund's point of view, or to clarify any points. Later, they would compare notes to see if their opinions about the Bund or Hitler had been changed.

21
Letters to Officials

November 26, 1937, Friday

True to his word, George Holmes prepared letters to send to the president, the governor, congressmen, and senators. He scrutinized all of the signatures on the original resolution pages from the mass meeting to copy down all of the names. This proved to be a difficult job since some of the writing was almost illegible. However, he did the best he could.

Holmes put together a packet to mail to President Franklin D. Roosevelt. The envelope would contain a cover letter, a typed version of the resolution and the pages of original signatures.[1] The letter told of the mass meeting in Southbury and how the resolution was unanimously adopted. Holmes stated that Congress had spent too much time just investigating Nazism, Communism, and Fascism. He urged officials to get to work to draft laws now and stop the spread of alien philosophies across America.

George Holmes' missive then went off track a bit, complaining about the members in Congress who were not interested in drafting legislation against the invaders. Holmes stated, "These men have no place in the halls of Congress as representatives of a free and independent people, if they are deficient in the mental capacity to analyze world events of the past twenty years, and to realize that eternal vigilance is the prices of our liberty and security against the insidious invasion of alien influence."

In closing, Holmes wrote, "Feeling assured that you will measure up to the full stature of an American, we now leave this matter in your hands." Being a practical person, Holmes made copies of the typed letter, and hand-wrote the name of the recipients. Holmes received replies from dozens of the officials, telling him to keep up the good work.

22
Article Stirs Up Town

November 28, 1937, Sunday

Once again Southbury citizens starting their morning reading a disturbing article in the *Waterbury Republican*. In large letters, the "Oath to Hitler" was printed on the front page. The German-American Bund members are required to quote this oath:

> I solemnly swear fidelity to my leader, Adolf Hitler. I promise Adolf Hitler and everybody designated by him ... the respect and absolute obedience due him and give allegiance to fulfill all orders without restrictions, and with my entire will...[1]

Those in town who thought the Bund was harmless, took notice of the idea that the Bund would bring the Nazi philosophy into town. While some might not be against the camp itself, the idea of the Bund being under Hitler's control and demanding their "absolute obedience without restrictions" was worse than they could imagine.

Adding to the agitation and uncertainty, a connection between the Bund in Southbury and a magazine thriller was brought up. The story, "Kingdom Come" by Martin McCall, was about a fictional organization similar to the Bund, who rose up to take over the United States. Upon a signal, the fictional "Red Sleeves" from the story suddenly commandeered the telephone lines, power plants, dams, all transportation systems, and the entire military. This take-over of the government happened within a few minutes after the alert because the internal structures were already in place. "America for Americans" was their battle cry.[2]

While that story was fictional, it seemed to follow the pattern of the Bund activities. This included establishing camps in strategic points close to factories; drilling troops and infiltrating spies and agents throughout businesses and government. If Southbury residents had not compared the Bund to the Nazis or the Red Sleeves before this moment, they fearfully did now.

After frightening the readers with the dire opening lines, the newspaper then offered hope, reminding the readers of ongoing investigations. Representative Samuel Dickstein of New York was still following the growth of the German-American Bund since it began and constantly reported to Congress on any new developments.

Also covered was an early study of Nazi organizations in American. Frank C. Hanighen found that the Bund seemed to be based on a foreign government and they were taking orders from abroad. While it was not a direct attack on the American government, the constant praise of Hitler's government was an indirect attack.[3]

Earlier in 1937, Attorney General Homer S. Cummings had directed the Federal Bureau of Investigation to look into the Bund camps to see if they were violating any federal laws. He especially wanted to know if they were shipping unregistered firearms across state lines.[4]

The leader of the Bund, Fritz Kuhn, welcomed a federal inquiry. A much-quoted statement from September 1937 was revived because it was relevant to the situation. "We are strictly an American organization with no connections with Germany. We DO show the Nazi emblem alongside of the American flag, with the biggest respect for Hitler and his movement in Germany."

Southbury had a lot to think about on this fall morning.

November 28, 1937, Sunday Afternoon

Even though heavy rain pelted the area, several town officials and spectators stopped by the campsite to check on the Bund's activities. Just days before, Westport Connecticut Bund member Erhard Frost stated that 200 members would be working this Sunday. He worked as a contractor and served on the Bund building committee. Frost was instrumental in gathering workers and tools for the Sunday work day.

While Route 6 was passable, the dirt roads were a muddy mess after three inches of rain flooded the roadways. The Bund leaders decided to cancel the work day at the campsite due to the rain and wet ground.

This was the second week in a row the Bund members did not work on clearing their property. Neighbor David Roulston confirmed that the workers failed to appear.

23
Wilhelm Kunze Visits Southbury

November 28, 1937, Sunday Afternoon

Wilhelm Kunze arrived at the parsonage in South Britain in the early afternoon, along with another man. Rev. Lindsay watched as the men exited the automobile. He was happy to see they wore nicely tailored suits. He had feared his visitors would arrive in Nazi-like uniforms.

Wilhelm Kunze introduced himself and his companion as *Herr* Schmidt, saying he was the treasurer of the Stamford Bund unit. Wilhelm Kunze extended greetings on behalf of his boss, the *Bundesführer*, Fritz Kuhn.

Lindsay escorted his guests into his study. The atmosphere was tense, as neither side knew exactly what to expect of the other. After all, the newspapers around the country had reported details of Rev. Lindsay's sermon calling the Bund "an insidious menace" and "an Un-American organization." How would a man who said such strong things about the Bund treat its representatives?

Lindsay drew from his Southern roots and rules of hospitality to put the two visitors at ease. He offered beverages and snacks to the travelers. After refreshments arrived and the small talk was ending, Lindsay confessed to the men that having so many reporters in town over the last week was a hardship to everyday life. He said he had answered reporter's questions but refused to talk on the radio. He felt that media twisted his answers. Lindsay was not sure he wanted to talk to any more reporters. Lindsay picked up his pad of paper in order to take notes. He encouraged his guests to begin.

Wilhelm Kunze thanked the pastor for meeting with them and assured him that the Bund coveted the respect and support of both Reverends Lindsay and Manley. In time, they would discover both the Bund and town were only trying to serve the best interests of the country, defending the same basic ideals and same opponents.

Kunze stated that Southbury was chosen for the honor of having the camp because of their loyalty to George Washington. "We call the Connecticut camp, Camp General von Steuben, after the man who made George Washington's military success possible. This is a great honor for Southbury to host the camp." Baron Friedrich von Steuben was a German officer who came to teach Washington's soldiers military discipline and the fighting skills to be able to beat the British forces.

Rev. Lindsay nodded with understanding. It was just five years ago when Southbury held a giant celebration to mark Washington's 200th birthday and his journey through town during the Revolutionary War. Special recognitions and events happened in various locations. The highlight was a large parade marching from the town hall in South Britain to Mansion House Road, even including Main Street. First Selectman Ed Coer was the grand marshal. The state police rerouted traffic around the town for the day. In the end, it was calculated the event brought in 10,000 people from all over the region.

Wilhelm Kunze went on to explain the purpose of Camp von Steuben was strictly to remove the children from the big cities during the summer to a place with fresh air. The camp would provide plenty of room to exercise the children's minds and bodies. He promised "there will not be any military training or drilling, because we are not a private militia," as some newspapers were reporting.

"Will the campers wear uniforms with swastikas?" ask Lindsay.

Herr Kunze answered: "There will be uniforms in the fashion of what Boy Scouts would wear. But only the uniformed security guards will wear a swastika patch."

Rev. Lindsay raised his eyebrow: "Security guards? Why would you need security guards at a camp?"

"We need them to direct traffic. When the camp is running next summer, we plan to have 1,000 campers per day, and up to 10,000 visitors on the weekends," said *Herr* Kunze. "In two of other camps, Camp Nordland and Camp Seigfried, we have had over 17,000 guests on one day. Camp General von Stueben is even larger and can accommodate more people." *Herr* Kunze continued to explain that the camp would eventually be used only for Connecticut groups of the Bund. Right now there were only two established Bund units in the state, but there would be more soon.

"Some of the neighbors are worried about the value of their property," said Lindsay.

"They do not understand," said Kunze. "The land values will increase. Bund families will buy the land in town because they want to be near the camp and all the activities. Just like at Camp Siegfried."

Kunze went on to explain that the farmers will benefit from the camp, because the camp would buy milk and produce from Southbury. Also, all of the building supplies would be locally sourced. Plus, the Bund needed specialized workers to help with construction and men to build a dam to create the 5-acre pond. Even the gas stations will have more cars stopping for gas. "Everyone will be happy that we chose this property," said Kunze.

Herr Schmidt added, "We are good neighbors. Tell your people that."

Lindsay had more questions. "Will the camp fly the swastika flag?"

"Yes, alongside the American flag."

"Why?"

"The Bund believes in the philosophy of Adolf Hitler, which represents no threat to American Democracy. We accept his interpretation of racial loyalty and kinship, and we look to Germany for our inspiration."

"But you are not under the control of Hitler?"

"Of course not. We are strictly an American organization, with no connection to the German government."

Lindsay found it interesting that a man who recently returned from a widely-publicized speaking engagement at the Nazi *Auslanders* meeting in Stuttgart could say the Bund had no connection with the German government. Lindsay kept silent, allowing Kunze to speak his piece.

"Of course we do not expect you to agree with us in everything at this stage," said Kunze. "But we expect the same American tolerance which is applied to others."

Their two-hour appointment came to an end and the men rose to leave. In parting, Kunze said, "I know that as we become better acquainted with each other, we will find nothing insurmountable in the way of friendly cooperation."

Lindsay was not sure if that was meant as a promise or a threat. But he thought of one last question. "Why was the camp project kept a secret from the town?"

Kunze answered simply, "We didn't want the Jews to prevent the sale."

Wilhelm Kunze and *Herr* Schmidt left Rev. Lindsay and went across town to visit Reverend Felix Manley of the Federated Church. The same basic material was discussed and the questions were answered the same way.[1]

The next day, Reverends Lindsay and Manley met to compare notes about their time with Wilhelm Kunze and *Herr* Schmidt. The pastors decided the visit with Kunze and Schmidt did not change their viewpoint of the German-American Bund in any way. They agreed it was un-American and something they did not want in Southbury. The pastors decided to continue working against the Bund camp project.[2]

Above left: Federated Church of Southbury, where Rev. Manley was the pastor in 1937. (*Southbury Historical Society*)

Above right: South Britain Congregational Church, Rev. Lindsay's church. (*Southbury Historical Society*)

Victorian Bridge across Lake Zoar. (*Southbury Historical Society*)

Lake Zoar as seen from Lakeside property. (*Soule Roberts Advertisement*)

Sign to the Lakeside "Restricted Community." (*Southbury Historical Society*)

Community Hall built of lumber collected before Lake Zoar was flooded.

Fritz Kuhn, Bund Leader in America beginning in 1936. (*Outtake March of Time, USHMM*)

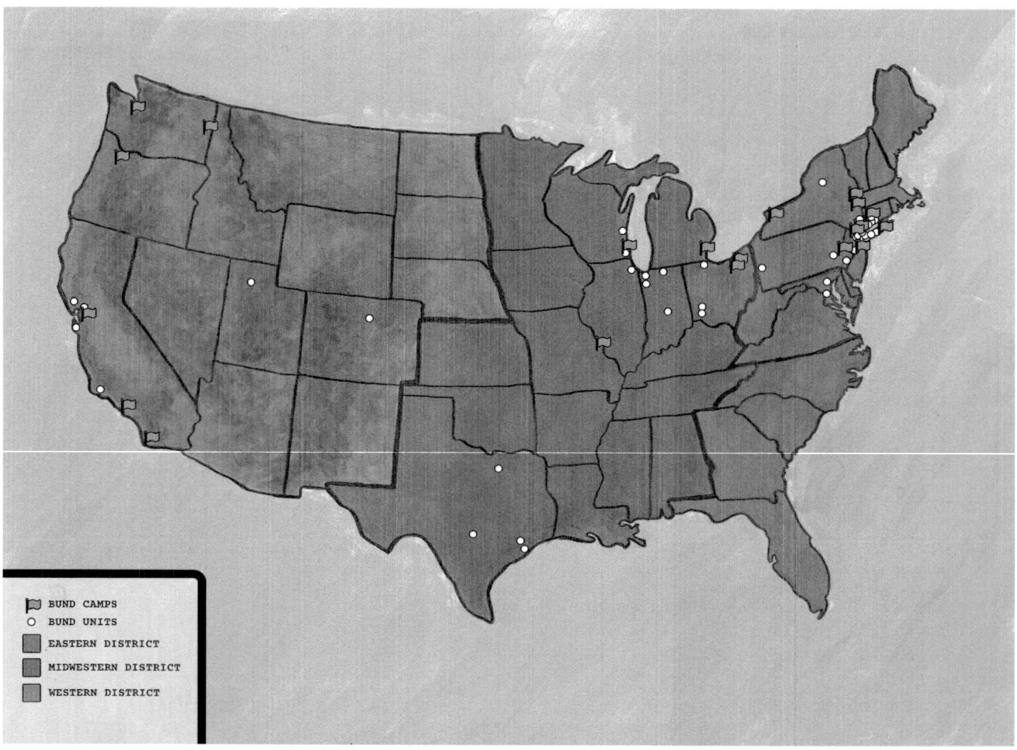

Map of Bund Regions and Camps. (*Drawn by Stephen Colon*)

German American Bund

UNIT:

ADDRESS:
GERMAN AMERICAN BUND
P. O. BOX 75, STATION "K"
New York, N. Y.

Application for Membership

DISTRICT: ....

UNIT: ....

Please do not use this space

No. ....

*) Payable when applying

Initiation Fee $1.00
Monthly Dues $0.75
Voluntary Donation $0.50 up

I hereby apply for admission to membership in the "German American Bund" the purposes and aims of which are known to me, and I obligate myself to support them to the best of my ability. I recognize the leadership principle, in accordance to which the Bund is being directed. I am of Aryan origin, free from jewish or colored blood.

Please write distinctly.

Full Name: .... Occupation: ....

German-American Bund application form. (*Southbury Historical Society*)

Camp Nordland. (*Southbury Historical Society*)

PURPOSE and AIMS

German American Bund

(AMERIKADEUTSCHER VOLKSBUND)

An Organization of Patriotic Americans of German Stock.

Left: Purpose and aims of the German-American Bund. (*Southbury Historical Society*)

Below: Fritz Kuhn meets Adolf Hitler. (*Souvenir Postcard from Amerikadeutscher Volksbund – Olympiafahrt 1936*)

Henry McCarthy's store, where the Bund members asked about supplies. (*Southbury Historical Society*)

Gas station where reporter saw the Bund members. (*Southbury Historical Society*)

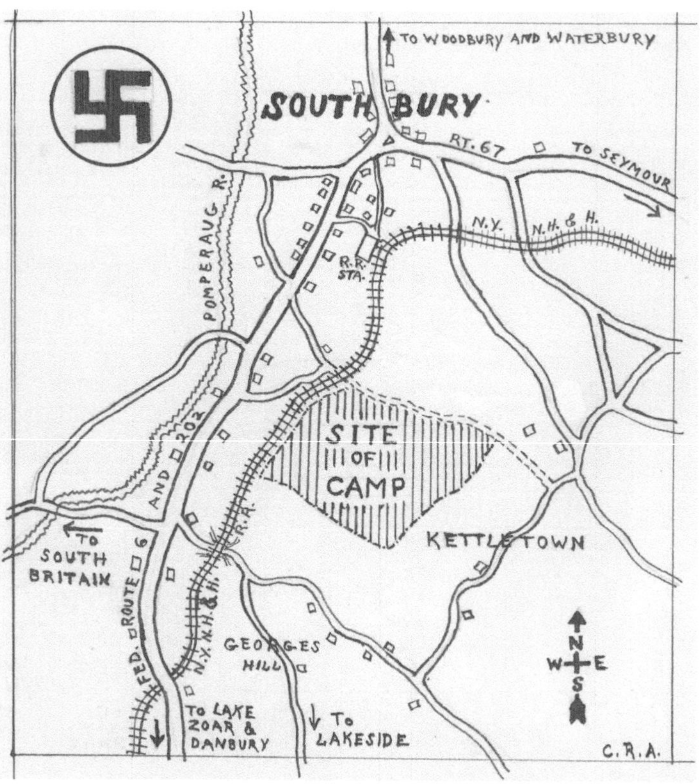

Above: Bund members working at campsite. (*Courtesy of the Republican-American*)

Left: Newspaper drawing of map to locate campsite, by C. Robert Abbott. (*Courtesy of the Republican-American*)

Every Citizen and Resident of
Southbury

ATTENTION!

The attached article describes an organization which purposes to overrun YOUR town.

Please read it and then decide whether or not you want the swastika and goose step thrust upon you, whether you want your land values depressed.

If you do not want these things, which the German-American Bund carries with it everywhere, attend the Town Meeting next Tuesday afternoon and do your civic duty.

The Kettletowners

Kettletowners' dire warning. (*Carol Plecan, from Ed Coer's Scrapbook*)

Above left: First Selectman J. Edward Coer. (*Courtesy of his daughter, Carol Plecan*)

Above right: Old town hall.

Above left: Alrick Nelson, grand juror. (*Courtesy of Lorraine Cable*)

Above right: Arresting Bund members, John King on right. (*Bridgeport Telegram*)

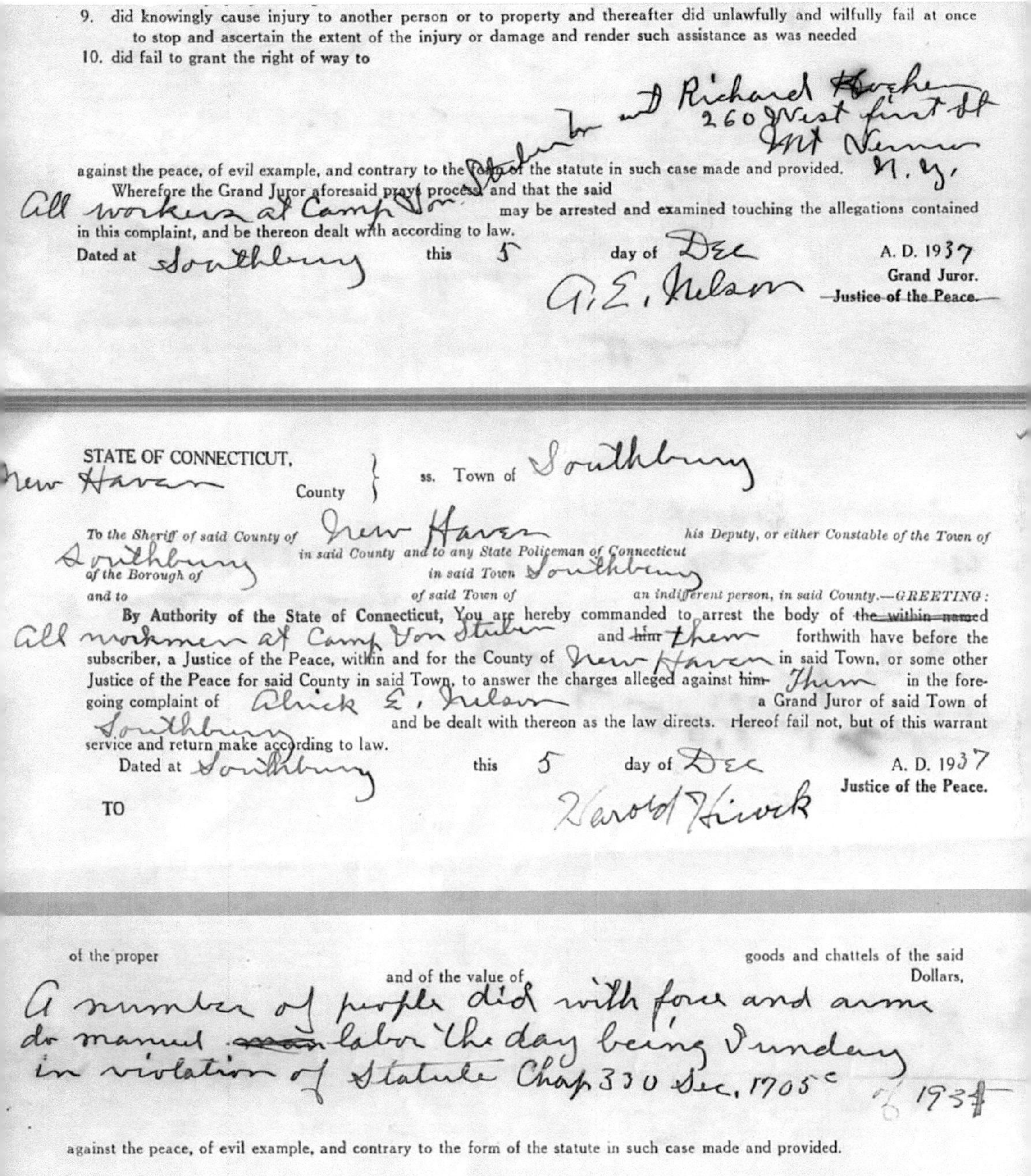

9. did knowingly cause injury to another person or to property and thereafter did unlawfully and wilfully fail at once to stop and ascertain the extent of the injury or damage and render such assistance as was needed

10. did fail to grant the right of way to

Richard ~~Hocher~~
260 West first St
Mt Vernon
N. Y.

against the peace, of evil example, and contrary to the form of the statute in such case made and provided.

Wherefore the Grand Juror aforesaid prays process and that the said All workers at Camp Von Steuben may be arrested and examined touching the allegations contained in this complaint, and be thereon dealt with according to law.

Dated at Southbury this 5 day of Dec A. D. 1937

A. E. Nelson Grand Juror.

~~Justice of the Peace.~~

STATE OF CONNECTICUT,
New Haven County } ss. Town of Southbury

To the Sheriff of said County of New Haven *his Deputy, or either Constable of the Town of* Southbury *in said County and to any State Policeman of Connecticut of the Borough of in said Town* Southbury *and to of said Town of an indifferent person, in said County.—GREETING:*

By Authority of the State of Connecticut, You are hereby commanded to arrest the body of ~~the within named~~ All workmen at Camp Von Steuben and ~~him~~ them forthwith have before the subscriber, a Justice of the Peace, within and for the County of New Haven in said Town, or some other Justice of the Peace for said County in said Town, to answer the charges alleged against ~~him~~ Them in the foregoing complaint of Alrick E. Nelson a Grand Juror of said Town of Southbury and be dealt with thereon as the law directs. Hereof fail not, but of this warrant service and return make according to law.

Dated at Southbury this 5 day of Dec A. D. 1937

Harold Hiirck Justice of the Peace.

TO

of the proper goods and chattels of the said and of the value of Dollars,

A number of people did with force and arms do manual ~~work~~ labor the day being Sunday in violation of Statute Chap 330 Sec. 1705c of 1937

against the peace, of evil example, and contrary to the form of the statute in such case made and provided.

General arrest warrant for Bund members. (*Southbury Historical Society*)

Above left: George Holmes in his tiny office at the gas station. (*Courtesy of the Republican-American*)

Above right: George Holmes' gas station. (*Courtesy of Bill Mc Allister*)

Above left: Gerhard Wilhelm Kunze. (*National Archives and Records Administration*)

Above right: Reverend M. E. N. Lindsay. (*Southbury Historical Society*)

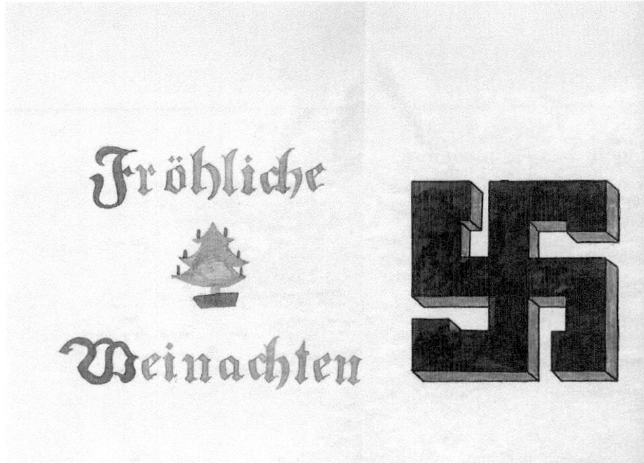

Above left: Home of Reverend M. E. N. Lindsay in 1937. (*Southbury Historical Society*)

Above right: Christmas greetings from Wilhelm Kunze to Rev. Lindsay. (*Southbury Historical Society*)

Right: Judge Hicock's home at Pine Hill and Route 6.

Judge Hicock's gas station near the community hall. (*Southbury Historical Society*)

Protestors Ernest Moeller and Richard Harrison. (*Courtesy of the Republican-American*)

Fritz Kuhn, Wilhelm Kunze, and Carl Nicolay. (*Outtake from March of Time, USHMM*)

German-American Bund Rally. (*Outtake from March of Time, USHMM*)

Above left: Blue Laws charges dropped, Judge Hicock, seated. (*Courtesy of the Republican-American*)

Above right: Miss Jennie Hinman at home in Southbury. (*Southbury Historical Society*)

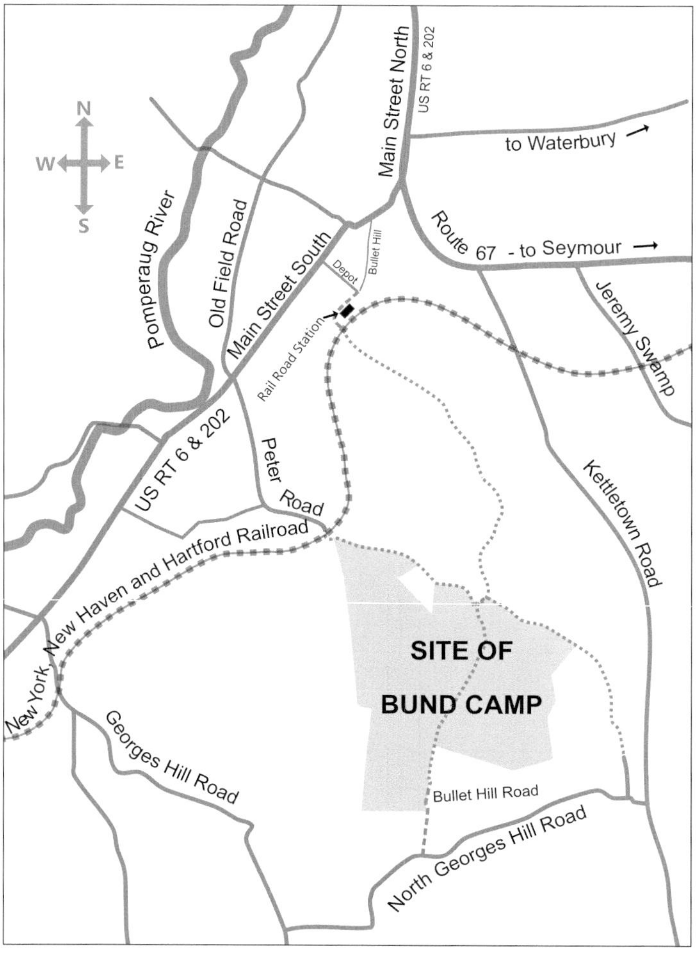

Accurate map locating Camp General Von Steuben based on Southbury Land Records. (*Image by Ray Elliott*)

24
Albert Aston Spills the Beans

November 29, 1937, Monday

A warning for another special town meeting was called by the selectmen for December 14, at 2 p.m., at the Southbury Community Hall. The purpose would be "To consider and act upon zoning regulations. All citizens and interested persons will have an opportunity to be heard in relation to zoning regulations."

Even though the town officials had been very careful to squash the idea that the zoning code was being presented because of Camp General von Steuben, Attorney Albert Aston, the chairman of the zoning commission, gave a statement to the contrary: "We are not trying to make believe that the commission has nothing to do with the camp." He stated everyone knew the panic about the camp was the reason zoning was being pushed through now. However, the commission was going to do a good job of zoning for the benefit of everyone and in alignment with other local town zoning codes. He warned there was some concern that the zoning regulations might not prevent the Bund from continuing with their plans. There was an urgency to pass the code before a building was constructed on the land.[1]

At Camp Nordland in New Jersey, the town enacted a zoning code against building on the land. However, they were too late. Since there were already a structures on the land, the whole camp had to be grandfathered in, allowing the buildings and the camp to stay. Zoning was only the first step in the Southbury official's plan. In reality, they feared the possibility of a long, drawn-out battle with Bund. Some people speculated that the town placed an attorney at the head of the Zoning commission to prevent legal loopholes in the new regulations.

Another reason the zoning code needed to be passed as soon as possible was that the land was currently owned by one individual, Wolfgang Jung. He had said at some point, the property would be turned over to the Bund when the organization was incorporated in the state. In the meantime, only the property holder was allowed to speak at the town meeting. He was allowed one vote, just like any other resident or land owner.

November 30, 1937, Tuesday

Opinions about how Southbury was handling the Bund continued to be published all over the country. *The Baltimore Sun*, a newspaper in Maryland, weighed in about the situation in Southbury. They reported the Nazi German-American Bund chose Southbury for a camp to cultivate devotion to Hitler and his philosophies. Even though the Bund wanted to turn the Yankees into Nazis, they never counted on Southbury fighting back.

The newspaper continued saying that if the Bund wanted to take over the country, they would have to outsmart some sharp-witted people like those in Connecticut.

25

The Annoying Visitors

November 29, 1937, Monday

Unknown to the pastors, or anyone else in town, Wilhelm Kunze and *Herr* Schmidt planned to stay in the Southbury for several days. Their goal was to convince as many residents as possible that Camp General von Steuben would be a benefit to the town. Kunze wanted to make sure there would be no more public objections to the camp.

Strangely, Kunze told some people that his name was Mr. Pulinze from Philadelphia, in charge of the Bund's publicity. Kunze was indeed from Philadelphia and the leader of publicity. His colleague was introduced as Mr. Schmidt, the Bund treasurer out of Stamford. The truth was Mr. Schmidt was actually Kurt Saher, a member of the Nazi party who was working quietly in a Jewish firm in New York City.[1] Kunze and Schmidt decided to track down all of the town officials to talk with them individually. Their first stop would be the town hall.

Later in the day, a car full of Bund members arrived in Southbury. They met up with Wilhelm Kunze to get their assignments. This group of local Bund members would stay on Main Street for the afternoon to meet and talk with the residents. They visited with men in the gas stations, and hung around outside the restaurants and the post office.

The Bundist's message was clear. The Bund was not un-American, nor were they Nazis; the camp would be just a camp, without any military-type drilling, and anyone who said otherwise was being misled by Jewish propaganda.

While Southbury residents found the Bund members tiresome, there were no disturbances around town. However, they were happy when the car load of men left.

Wilhelm Kunze and *Herr* Schmidt returned to their hotel for another night.

November 30, 1937, Tuesday

Before leaving the Bund headquarters in New York City, Wilhelm Kunze arranged to information about the German-American Bund mailed to all the households in Southbury. They were expected to start arriving in mailboxes on Tuesday. When the residents opened their mailbox that morning, they found a brown envelope with a pamphlet inside. On the cover were the words *Purpose and Aims* directly above the swastika sign of the German-American Bund. Also enclosed was a German-

American Bund "Application for Membership." In order to join the Bund, the following statement had to be approved and signed by the prospective member:

> I hereby apply for admission to membership in the "German-American Bund" the purposes and aims of which are known to me, and I obligate myself to support them in the best of my ability. I recognize the leadership principle, in accordance to which the Bund is being directed. I am of Aryan origin, free from jewish or colored blood.[2]

Receiving a mass mailing from the Kettletowners was one thing, but receiving mail from the Bund was quite disturbing.

On this morning, and the next day, car loads of Bund members arrived to meet with Wilhelm Kunze. While Kunze continued to reach out to town officials, the Bund members would spread across the town to convince the town they were nice guys.

On the way to school, children were stopped by Bund members. The men were friendly and polite, handing out official *Amerikadeutscher Volksbund* arm patches to the children and youth. The patch was red and white with a yellow swastika sprouting up from a rising sun the letters AV in the half-circle. The children were encouraged to sew the emblem onto their jackets. They were invited to visit the camp whenever they wanted because the Bund had nothing to hide.[3]

When the parents found out, they were furious their children were approached by the Bund members. Parents and teachers alike warned the children to walk in pairs and to go home immediately after school. Above all, they were not to talk with strangers.[4]

George Holmes pointed out if the camp was established, there would be people in Nazi uniforms roaming up and down the streets of town all the time. He warned that the low morals of Nazi youth could even spread to the town's children.

A car with several Bundist went to find Rev. Lindsay. He and his wife had gone up to Waterbury with their youngest daughter on a shopping trip. When the Bund members did not find him at home, they went over to the church which was next to the South Britain Schoolhouse. Two of his daughters attended the school. When the men inquired about Rev. Lindsay, his girls were pointed out by the others. After one look at the men, Lois told Joanie to run. They ran and hid behind the church until the men left.[5]

Southbury's young men were drawn to the visiting Bund members, wanting to learn everything they could about the organization. With the limited number of jobs in town due to the depression, the young men were attracted to the possibility of working for the Bund. The town parents were concerned their sons would be enticed by the Nazi propaganda and join the organization.

Several craftsmen in town made agreements with the Bund to handle specialty work. One was Amos Ewing Barclay, an electrician and a cabinet maker. While he didn't care much for the Bund's politics, he appreciated the work.

Southburians were very disturbed at the pushiness of the Bund organization and were ready to rebel. When the Bund members starting going door to door to meet the residents, they did not find many who were willing to talk with them.

The Bund representatives found themselves under constant observation by the locals as they tried to drum up support and tradesmen to help with the camp construction. While they did not seem to be dangerous, their presence everywhere annoyed the townspeople. More than once the Grand Juror, Alrick Nelson, received a call to investigate a complaint against the Bund. The state policeman, the sheriff, and constables also received complaints. The law enforcers decided to have a visible presence along Main Street, by patrolling and just being seen.

Kunze spent the first part of the week trying to woo the town officials, then resorted to making "dire threats." However, First Selectman Ed Coer reported that "None of the officials seemed to scare very much."[6]

A group calling themselves "One Hundred Percent Americans" held rallies in various parts of town to protest the Bund members. They organized a parade specifically aimed to antagonize the Bund members. The group sent a card to Rev. Lindsay, complaining about the Bund:

> If they don't like our country let them go back to Germany. They have no right to establish training camps here to keep physically fit to resume military service for Germany when recalled for that purpose. Furthermore, they should not be permitted to carry on their pernicious propaganda.
>
> One Hundred Percent Americans[7]

The situation could have easily gotten out of hand, but fortunately cooler heads prevailed. The Bund members finally departed Southbury leaving families frazzled, but determined. If Wilhelm Kunze thought his persuasion tactics would win over the town, he was very wrong. The residents were more than ready to get rid of the pro-Nazi Bund from Southbury through legal means.

26

Alrick Nelson Makes a Move

December 5, 1937, Sunday

Grand Juror Alrick Nelson had reached his limit. The previous week had been very frustrating with Wilhelm Kunze and his cohorts in town. In his position as the grand juror, Nelson had received dozens of calls accusing Bund members of various offenses. Even though the Bund members pushed the limits, they had broken no laws that could lead to an arrest.

There was no doubt the Bund members would return today to continue clearing trees for the camp site, but after the tensions of last week, Nelson was not sure how the town would react.

Alrick Nelson became a grand juror in 1923. It is an appointed position, made by the town judge who ruled on criminal cases. Currently, Harold Hicock held the position as the judge. Nelson was chosen because of his level head and strict adherence to the law. The grand juror investigates complaints to decide if a law has been violated. If so, they fill out the arrest warrant which is then signed by the judge.

As expected, the Bund members arrived again to clear their land. The now-hypervigilant neighbors and observant residents called Juror Alrick Nelson to complain about the noise and the fact the Nazis were back. They were ready to file written complaints against the Bund. Nelson made the short trek from his house to see for himself what was happening and found about thirty men working on removing trees and stumps.

Nelson drove into town to see Justice of the Peace Harold Hicock at his home next to the Federated Church. After a short examination of the complaints, they decided it was time to take action. Nelson wrote out numerous "John Doe" warrants to arrest Bund members which Judge Hicock promptly signed. They decided it was appropriate to use the state law that prohibited work on Sunday.

> Did with force and arms do labor on Sunday prohibited by Statute of 1935 Chapter 330, Section 1705C.[1]

Even though it was viewed as an ancient "Blue Law," the latest revision of the law was written only two years previously.

After church services and Sunday dinner were over, Nelson gathered the town constables, which included John B. King, David S. Joselwitz, Norman Beardsley, Frank Bower, Edward A. Scoville, and John Walker. Climbing into three vehicles, the group went up to the camp site where the Bund members were working. As they pulled into the clearing, they recognized a few newspaper reporters and photographer milling around the Bund workers.[2] Constable John B. King, who was a robust and congenial real estate agent, jumped out of the car and loudly announced, "You are all under arrest for working on a Sunday." Everyone stopped what they were doing to see what was going on. Constable King spied Gustav Korn with a pick ax in his hand, where he had been removing the roots of a young tree and strode over to him. "My name is King. I'm a constable in this town and I have a warrant for your arrest." The photographers ran over to get photographs of the action.

A man protested, "Can't we clear the trees away and make a picnic ground and recreation camp here if we want to?" The constable answered they could any day of the week except Sunday. He wrote down Korn's name on a warrant and saw Robert Koehler pulling down a tree with a rope. Constable King scribbled down his name, and Koehler was also arrested.[3]

Chaos broke out as the Bund members pushed forward and all started talking at once, protesting the arrests. Comments of "We didn't know we were breaking the law," and "No one warned us this was illegal," rang out. The constables stood firm, not engaging in the arguments. Even though they arrived with dozens of warrants, they had not planned how they would arrest everyone who was working. Alrick Nelson said they actually saw the two men in action and their arrest was enough to get the point across.

When asked by the Bund members what would happen next, Constable King stated that the two must either post bond or they would be taken to the jail in Seymour. The Bundist protested, and Alrick Nelson made the decision to move the accused off of the Bund's land and away from the now angry crowd. Korn and Koehler were loaded into the car with Nelson and King and they headed toward town. The constables followed. Bund members and reporters raced to their cars to catch up with the constable's cars. Their destination was Judge Hicock's house at the corner of Pine Road and Route 6, where the judge usually heard cases on Saturday.

All the while, Wolfgang Jung sat on a stump and watched the scene unfold. He did not volunteer the fact that he was the legal owner of the property. Nor did he go to town with the other Bund members. He was asked by a reporter to make a statement, but he declined any comment.

At Judge Hicock's house, it was discovered the judge was not there and someone was sent to get him. He was working at his garage near the Community Hall. The room was quickly crowded, and many of the Bund members decided to stand outside instead. Mrs. Hicock removed her children from living room and sent them away to a quieter part of the house.[4]

While waiting for the judge to arrive, the Bund members protest bitterly, saying that their work was recreational and not labor. They had not intended to break any law. Others volunteered they had seen something unusual that day. Two airplanes were seen flying low over the campsite and circled around several times. The planes were low enough the workers could see pictures were being taken of their activities.

27
Judge Hicock Decides

December 5, 1937, Sunday afternoon

Judge Hicock arrived home from his gas station garage where he had been repairing a car. After surveying the situation at his house, Hicock, who was dressed in boots and a heavy coat, excused himself to get cleaned up. Eventually returning to sit at his desk, he listened to the grand juror explain the situation. Both Korn and Koehler sat in front of the judge, not entering a plea of guilty or not guilty. The men said they were working with others at the camp, but no one knew that they were breaking the law. Korn, a cabinet maker by trade, stated, "I was caught red-handed. I'll serve two or three years in jail if necessary. I don't care. It's all a racket."

Judge Hicock refused a request to pass immediate judgement. He said that the issue was of intense public interest and much too important to settle immediately. He set a trial date for the next Saturday, December 11 at 10 o'clock in the Community Hall.

The judge declared that the bond was $75 per person, to be paid immediately or the men would be taken directly to jail. When the two men refused to pay $75 each, Judge Hicock gave them the choice between the jail in Seymour and the one in New Haven.[1] Neither man had the funds with them. Word was passed to bund members inside and out, who contributed their pocket money until $150 was reached. The bund members pushed into the house to see if enough money had been raised. It took a while for the constables to count the money, as it was mostly in small bills and coins.

Seeing the crowd at Justice Hicock's house, several Southbury residents stopped to see what was going on. A lively discussion broke out among the Bund members and residents. Alrick Nelson asked the Bund members why they thought they could "organize in this country to try to overthrow the government." Many of them laughed and asked, "Who said we wanted to do that?" One unidentified Bund member, who refused to give his name, because he worked for a Jewish company and did not want his association with the Bund exposed, said, "You have been misled by Jewish propaganda." Several townspeople recognized him as *Herr* Schmidt who had stayed in town the previous week with Wilhelm Kunze.

The workers stated that they were just trying to build a camp for recreation, and attempted to explain the purposes and goals of the German-American Bund. "We are just as good and law-abiding citizens of this country as anyone in this town." John B. Unkel, a chauffeur out of Larchmont, New York, claimed he served in the United States Army during the war. "I was an officer fighting against the Germany," he said. "Do you think I would join an un-American group?"

Many Bund members chimed in with their story. "I have ancestors who came to America as early as those of anyone here in Southbury," claimed a young man. "Most of us were born here and all of us are American citizens," said another.

The discussion was friendly and at no time did anyone display anger or any violent emotions. "We'll all be on friendly terms once the town understands the truth about our organization and the good it will do to the town to have the camp here." Appearing to speak for the group, *Herr* Schmidt continued. "We came here to build a large camp and bring business to this town." In a wheedling tone, Schmidt continued. "We have $800 to pay local workers to build a dam for our five-acre swimming pool." He continued saying that there was other work to be done before the campers arrive. And in the summer, they would purchase all of their food and supplies from local farmers and merchants.

His words, while friendly, then took on a slightly threatening tone. "Don't you folks realize what a blessing the camp will be for you? If you continue to stand in our way, we will just move to another location." He pointed out business was booming near other Bund camps, with the real estate values increasing 30 percent.

Mr. John Unkel, who had worked at the campsite since November 7, stated that the arrests would not stop the Bund from building the camp. "We will keep on working at this site. If we can't work on Sunday, we'll come up on Saturdays. We can come up on Friday night and be here all day Saturday. We might even build a building to stay overnight."[2]

Unkel was asked a question about how the zoning code would affect the Bund's plan for the camp. He did not seem to think they would be concerned at all, because other towns with camps had tried to pass zoning laws. "Whatever the town does, we will abide by it. If they make the land a residential area, we will not violate the regulation," he said. However, he did indicate that they might have ways of working around the code.

Nelson told the group that they were setting a bad example by working on Sundays. One Bund member asked why Judge Hicock was working on cars on a Sunday. The judge answered that it was a "reasonable exception to the law." The questioner indicated they thought that was just an excuse by the judge, but Hicock opened his law book and showed the statute with the exception in the law that made it legal for car repairs to be done on Sunday.[3]

Another claimed they saw many farmers working out in the fields and demanded to press charges against them. Nelson said he would need the names of the farmers, and he would have to look into the charges if there was a complaint. However, it would take time, he said, because he would need to investigate and issue warrants. The matter was dropped.

The Bund members left town a little confused and with an interesting story to tell their leaders.

28

Blue Law Arrests Bitterly Opposed

December 6, 1937, Monday

If the Southbury residents had not heard about the arrest of two Bund members on Sunday, they would learn about it on Monday morning through the newspaper reports and the local gossip.

While some applauded the posse approach to justice, the majority of the people in town and throughout the country seemed to disapprove. During the week, opposition appeared in the newspapers, as well as tongue-lashings directly from the townspeople.

The most ominous disapproval came from the *Bundesführer* Fritz Kuhn, who sent a stern warning to Southbury. He threatened to have everyone in town arrested if they continued to oppose the establishment of the camp. Kuhn said they would press charges against every man and women who worked on Sunday. This would include every gas station worker, every farmer, everyone in a restaurant or hotel, and any other businesses that were open.[1]

In his disgust with Southbury, Kuhn reportedly threatened to sell the camp to the cult leader Father Divine. Connecticut had already had a run-in with Father Divine earlier in the year; he had tried to escape the law and hid within the state. In May 1937, he was extradited from Connecticut to face criminal charges in New York. Even though Father Divine was not someone Southbury wanted in town, Fritz Kuhn had made the same hollow threats against Camp Seigfried.[2]

Carl Nicolay, eastern organizer of the Bund, called the arrests ridiculous. He stated the work at the camp would continue, and threatened to start a lawsuit against Southbury. Nicolay said court action was unpleasant, but the Bund was prepared to fight for their rights. He was quick to add the Bund had already won several other lawsuits across the country against zoning. His hope, however, was that Southbury and the Bund could come to a mutual understanding.

The *Waterbury Republican* editor wrote an article called "The Wrong Means." He used this forum to show his dislike of the Blue Laws and the fact they were still active laws. He warned that they could be used as a legal means in a personally vindictive manner. While agreeing the Nazis were evil and should not be building a camp in Connecticut, the editor stated this was not the right means to solve the problem. In fact, the Blue Laws arrest could elicit sympathy for the Bund, virtually making them martyrs.

A *New York Times* editorial disapproved of the arrest tactics; they claimed—perhaps a little tongue-in-cheek—that Southbury should go about being themselves and let the Nazis be Nazis. However, the *Times* firmly believed that the Yankee spirit would prevail in the end.[3]

The verbal and written attacks against Grand Juror Alrick Nelson and Judge Harold Hicock protesting the arrest of the two Bund members swirled around town in a constant covering of discord. George Holmes, who was the first person reporters now turned to for an opinion, gave a very harsh response. He called the arrests unwarranted and a ridiculous action that amounted to persecution. Appearing to make a statement on behalf of the whole population of Southbury, Holmes said, "The townspeople of Southbury thoroughly disapprove of this action by raiding the camp without warning of any kind."

Holmes, who had been almost vicious in his letters to the editor and his resolutions against the pro-Nazi camp seemed to be taking an opposite stand on the arrests. He was quick to say the Bund members committed no crime and should not have been arrested. Holmes spoke with both Judge Hicock and Grand Juror Nelson to try to get them to drop the charges against the Bund members. He claimed he got nowhere, and the trial would still be held on Saturday.

Rev. Felix Manley of the Federated Church wrote, "An old Connecticut blue law was invoked to add a legal harassment to the verbal one with which Southbury has welcomed the Bundsters."[4]

Basil Bass, who planned to help Alrick Nelson prosecute the Bund members, stated that he personally never approved of the arrests based on the Blue Law. Alrick Nelson grew tired of all the complaints directed at him. In a letter to the town and to the editor of the *Waterbury Republican*, he asked the question, "What is a blue law?" He asked for someone to help him understand the controversy. If the law was too old to be used, why was it revised in 1935 by the State legislators? How could it be considered an "ancient" law? His stated that his job was to enforce the statutes, which was his sworn duty.[5] No matter what anyone else thought or said, Alrick Nelson would do the right thing, as dictated by the law.[6]

One Southbury clergyman spoke out, but did not want his name used in the newspaper. He said that he had polled his congregation and found that the sentiment of the townspeople was not favorable to using the Sunday blue law against the Bund. Whether the town had a sudden attack of Yankee fairness or feared the threatened retributions from the long arm of Hitler was never revealed.

29
Commission Reveals Zoning Code

December 8, 1937, Wednesday

Amazingly, a mere two weeks after the town voted for a zoning commission to come up with a zoning code, the document was completed. Attorney Albert Aston, released an advanced copy to town officials and the newspapers. In his cover letter, he reminded everyone that the code was not made to "be against any person or group of persons, but for the good of the town in general."

The Zoning Commission issued a statement saying that while drafting the zoning code, they were especially careful to take into account the history and beauty of the town. They stated the real estate values were largely based "upon the town's natural beauty, the colonial architecture, its pleasing aspect of the highways and its character as a historical New England town."[1]

The Zoning Commission's code divided the town into four districts with special categories of farming and residential; business; industrial; and recreational. The business districts were set along the main roads in Southbury center, South Britain, and Southford, with the only industrial property at the Hawkins factory. The recreational district was placed along Lake Zoar and the Pomperaug River.

Everything else fell under the farming and resident district. This includes "dwelling houses, farms, nurseries, greenhouses, churches, public schools, public museums, public or private libraries, public park, reservoirs, wells, water towers or water filter beds, roadside stand, professional offices in private homes, and accessory uses." The Bund land was categorized under the farm and residential district, and would not be allowed to build a camp on their property, because the land is not in a recreational district.

Within the code was a list of prohibited uses in Southbury. These included manufacture of explosive; storage of explosives in bulk; a slaughter house; penal institution; manufacturer of fertilizer; or "military training or drilling with or without arms except by the legally constituted armed forces of the United States, any of the several states, the territories of possessions of the United States or the legally constituted police forces thereof, or of any municipality thereof."[2] The regulations would become effective immediately after approving the code at a special town meeting. Any violations of the code would be subject to a penalty of $250.

A grandfather clause was added that allowed any use of land already existing or started, could continue. Stated as "A use existing at the time of adoption of these regulations which does not conform to the regulations herein may be continued, but shall not be extended." In other words, if a structure was already built on the Bund property, then the Bund could have continued with their additionally planned buildings.

30
United Americans Rise Up

December 10, 1937, Friday

George Holmes was committed to fight against anything un-American. With everything he had done recently, he felt he was waging a one-man war against the Hitler. After numerous speaking engagements at American Legion and veterans' organizations, he felt he had enough to support to form a group and share the load. His plan was to get the organization started, and then step back to be just one of the members. That is not exactly what happened.

The morning papers broke the news that Holmes was once a member of the Ku Klux Klan. According to people who worked with him at the Uniroyal Rubber

Company, he was a leader of the KKK, recruiting members in the plant. George Holmes claimed that he was only a member for two months, when he found out the real purposes of the KKK.[1]

Even though the newspapers made a big deal about Holmes' previous affiliation with the Ku Klux Klan, the subject was widely ignored in Southbury. Just a decade earlier, many of the Southbury town leaders and residents were part of the same organization.[2] That was a time the town preferred to forget at this point.

A neighbor of George Holmes reported a visitor arrived at the gas station to meet with Holmes. Several photographs were taken with the gentlemen, recognized as James W. Ford—who had run for vice president in 1936. Not only was he the first African-American to run for high office, he was a member of the Communist Party. George Holmes left with the former candidate and his photographer to visit the Bund camp site. The photographs were expected to be in the *Communist Trade Journal of New York*.[3]

No one seemed to care about the news at that evening's meeting. At 7:30 p.m., a crowd of over 100 people representing twenty towns were seated inside the Southbury Community Hall. They heard an overview of the organization that George Holmes hoped to form. It would be non-partisan and non-sectarian, with no initiation fee, no dues and no salaried officers. Holmes stated that the only way to eliminate and block Nazi activities was through legislation.

To prove the need for the organization, Holmes enlisted the support of many speakers. Dr. Emily Pierson from Cromwell, a state social worker, and member of the Connecticut League for Peace of Democracy, an off-shoot of the American Communist League, was a key speaker. She had recently traveled extensively in Germany. While there she asked many people how they felt about Hitler's regime. She reported that people refused to speak, but would write down their answers on a scrap of paper and immediately burned them after they were read. Dr. Pierson warned that allowing the Nazi camp would encourage Hitler's value to expand to Connecticut. Other speakers against the Nazis included Miss Eleanor Stevenson of New Milford; Miss Jennie Hinman, Albert Aston, Grand Juror Nelson, of Southbury; H. Rees El-Bara of New Haven, an officer of the Inter-Veteran's council of New Haven; and Milton H. Richmond, of Hartford.

The highlighted speaker was Miss Isobel Steele of Newtown, a former newspaper correspondent who spent four months in a German prison for her outspoken stance against the Nazis. She was loudly applauded by the audience. Miss Steele urged that every means be taken to eliminate the Nazi forces in America.

The newly established organization chose Holmes as the chief officer of the United American movement. Two Southbury residents were elected to be on the board. Robert J. Harrison became the sergeant and Mrs. Anita Darrot the secretary treasurer. Mrs. Darrot's husband was the head clock designer for Seth Thomas clocks.

The organization would be set up into three nationwide divisions with camps in each state, outposts in any community that wanted one, and a national headquarters.

Officers would include a commander, vice commander, recording secretary, corresponding secretary, treasurer, and a committee on Un-American activities.

Throughout the night, Jack Smith, a farmer dressed in his overalls, kept a running commentary while listening to the speakers. His comments were a source of encouragement to all around. "Let them try to beat us, if they can!" "Those Germans won't have half a chance when we get hot," and "We'll show them!"

The evening was interrupted when the door of the community hall flew opened to admit Edward Wallace. Walking down the aisle, he stopped halfway to give the Nazi salute and said, "I'm sick and tired of all this bunk! I'm for the Germans and I don't care who knows it." The group watched in shock, thinking that perhaps a Bund member had wandered into the meeting. Wallace walked over to the ladies at the side table and spoke in abusive and profane language.

Robert Harrison, the newly elected sergeant of the outpost, asked nicely for Wallace to leave. When Wallace refused, state policeman Santey and Constable David Joselwitz came to help. With the help of additional men, Wallace was carried through the swinging door. The door swung back and hit Wallace in the face, leaving a bleeding gash on his forehead.

While trying to place Wallace in the state police car, there was a scuffle, which caused some damage to the vehicle. Wallace was taken to a holding cell in Seymour where he was later released when a friend arrived to pay his bail. When the United Americans meeting continued, one man expressed regret that Wallace was ejected for speaking his mind. He proposed a motion that no one would be refused a voice who disagreed with the organization. Milton Richmond declared that too much fuss was given to the situation and said, "Forget about the drunken man." George Holmes suggested a pledge for the United Americans. After some discussion, it was approved.

The group decided to have a presence at the Bund trial the next day. Several members from out of town spent the night in Southbury. A few ambitious workers made picket signs to carry around the community hall before and after the trial.

31

Blue Law Trial

December 11, 1937, Saturday Morning

The day arrived for the trial of Bund members Gustav Korn and Richard Koehler, who were arrested the previous Sunday at the Bund camp site. The number of reporters who showed up for the trial was unprecedented for a local event. The town's inns were full to capacity with reporters who came to observe the battle between a small town and the German-American Bund. The Blue Laws Trial had caught the attention of the whole country.

To handle the needs of the news teams, additional telegraph lines were installed at the railroad depot. Western Union added a couple of boys to serve as runners to collect the news from the reporters and return to the telegraph office. The stories would be wired to the New York City papers and beyond.[1]

Since only a limited number of public telephones were available in the whole town, some reporters made special arrangements with the neighbors close to the Community Hall. The local's telephones were rented for an hour after the trial. Each reporter was hoping to be the first to have their story in their editor's hands.

Reporters arrived at the Community Hall at 9 a.m., an hour before the scheduled start of the trial. They represented a cross section of the media, both local and national. There were at least ten photographers, sixteen reporters, and three Pathé newsmen with a complete recording setup for newsreels. In spite of the heavy frost and bitter cold, the reporters waited outside, observing the activity as the people arrived. Several were coaxed to stop and talk with them.

Inside the Hall, the wood stove was working hard to warm the large room. Smoke leaked out of a hole in the stovepipe, filling the area with a light haze. A few windows were opened to let the smoke out, but instead, it let in more of the 10-degree air from outside.[2]

Grand Juror Alrick Nelson, who started his milk delivery route an hour early this day, arrived with Basil Bass, New York City attorney, at 9:30 a.m. They searched the crowd for Justice Harold Hicock. Not finding him there, they drove to his home.

The accused men, Richard Koehler of Mount Vernon, New York, and Gustav Korn of New Rochelle, New York, entered through the back door to avoid the reporters and photographers. With them was Duncan C. Folger of New Rochelle, leader of the Westchester and Bronx Bund districts. Wolfgang Jung, the owner of the campsite land, was also present. The crowd grew silent in anticipation as Koehler and Korn approached the tables at the front of the room.

The hall was used for many town functions. The stage was still set up from a recent play, which coincidently had a backdrop depicting a German castle on the Rhine River. The scenery was surrounded by local advertisements. Moments later, Justice Hicock arrived with Alrick Nelson and Basil Bass. After a short intense conversation with the accused, Hicock turned to address the spectators. He announced the trial was being postponed because material witnesses for the prosecution did not show up.

A discussion followed between the Southbury lawmen and the Bund members as to when the trial could be rescheduled. Bund leader Duncan Folger stated that the trial would have to wait until the German Exposition and Christmas Market was over on December 24, because all Bund members were involved in the events. The Monday after Christmas was chosen as the new trial date. The audience members were both shocked and greatly disappointed. Several heated discussions broke out around the room. The press took this opportunity to question the Bund members.

The accused men revealed they did not come with a lawyer to defend themselves. Mr. Korn declared that he did not want an attorney, and frankly stated that he was guilty of working on Sunday. "I like everyone up here in Southbury," said Mr. Korn. "I don't want to violate any law." He followed by saying he did not care about the outcome of the case. He was friendly and chatted with anyone who approached him. Korn seem to be offering himself as a martyr for the cause, while Mr. Koehler remained totally silent. Duncan Folger reported the Bund workers would not be returning to the campsite on Sunday, December 12. He said that no work could be attempted because the ground was frozen.

Outside the community hall, members of the newly-formed United Americans walked around with picket signs. Young Ernest Moeller, dressed in his work clothes, held a sign that said: "OLD GLORY IS OUR FLAG. SOUTHBURY WANTS NO SWASTIKA." While Robert Harrison marched with another sign which said: "UNITED AMERICANS SHOW THE WAY." And "NO NAZI CAMPS."[3]

When the bustle of people leaving the hall died down, the Pathé newsmen recorded short speeches by three of the protestors: Nelson H. Bellmay of Waterbury, along with George A. Holmes and Robert J. Harrison from Southbury. Mr. Bellmay declared the United American were founded "To fight the Nazi movement in America. Our first job is to keep them out of Southbury."

"There is no place in Southbury for divided Americanism," said Harrison.

Holmes, the organizer and leader of the new United Americans organization, said, "Southbury is an American town. We want the American flag, not the Swastika."[4] The interviews were shown on the Pathé newsreels in theaters across America.

The reporters were unhappy that their news story of the year turned out to be a bust, until they learned of a second trial. Edward Wallace, who was arrested at the United American's meeting the previous evening, would be tried at Judge Hicock's house at 2 p.m.[5] Since it was loosely related to the Bund situation, many reporters decided to attend.

Grand Juror Alrick Nelson left the community hall disturbed that the witnesses did not show up. He had thought they would attend after taking the trouble to write out official complaints against the Bund workers. He wondered if Fritz Kuhn's threats to shut down the town were the deterrent. Maybe they feared for their families and Southbury. Nelson vowed that next time he would make sure the witnesses were served subpoenas requiring them to testify.

32
The Kitchen Court

December 11, 1937, Saturday Afternoon, Judge Hicock's House

The reporters were disappointed that the trial of the century did not develop. They interviewed everyone they could and looked around for another story to send their editors. They decided it would be worth the time to spend a few more hours in Southbury to cover the second trial.

The accused was Edward S. Wallace, who served as a second lieutenant in the U.S. Air Force during the world war.[1] He was a graduate of Yale University and received a master's degree from Harvard.

Promptly at 1:30 p.m., a number of residents, and an equal number of reporters, sat in the living room of Judge Harold Hicock home, waiting for the trial to begin. When Hicock saw the large number of cameras, he told the photographers they "better lay low" and gave every indication he did not want any publicity for the Wallace case.

Trooper Santey arrived at 2 p.m. and asked to speak to Judge Hicock and Grand Juror Nelson. They walked into the kitchen with Mr. Wallace and shut the door. After a few moments, the reporters tried to open the door, but found it was locked. Some rattled the door, while others walked around the house to peak into a window to see what was happening. About five minutes later, Mr. Nelson came out, picked up his briefcase from off the table in the living room, and walked toward the door. "Where will the trial be held?" asked one reporter.

"It's all over," replied Mr. Nelson. Immediately, everyone started talking at once and verbally attacking Nelson for holding a secret trial. The reporters claimed that it was illegal to bar the public from a trial. Another quoted a General Statutes to that effect. Mr. Nelson listened to the comments silently. With a frown, he walked back into the kitchen. Within moments, Justice Hicock burst out of the kitchen and was immediately besieged with questions. A reporter asked, "What's this all about?"

The judge replied, "What's it to you?"

"Can we quote you saying that?" shouted one reporter.

"Go to it," said the justice. "I don't care." Asked when the trial would take place, Hicock said, "It's all taken care of." He volunteered no details. George Holmes happened to walk into the house during the middle of the commotion and demanded to know what was going on. The newspapermen quickly explained and Holmes turned to Hicock. "Why aren't you allowing the public to attend this trial?" he asked straight out. "Don't you realize you are holding an unconstitutional star-chamber session?"

Justice Hicock walked into the kitchen at the same time Wallace walked out. Wallace refused to discuss the trial, but he willingly told the reporters what he had done the night before. "It was liquor. Someone suggested to me that I go into the meeting and nominate Justice Hugo L. Black as president of the United Americans and I thought it was a good idea. I didn't really think you folks were serious about this business," he told Holmes.

Hicock and Nelson walked back into the living room and the justice sat down at his table. "Court's in session," he declared. Looking at Wallace, he said, "You are charged with breach of peace. How do you plead?'

"Guilty," Wallace replied.

"Court's over," the justice announced. The reporters were still not satisfied. "But aren't you going to fine the man?" one asked.

"He has already been fined," answered the justice.

"How much was it?" asked another reporter. Justice Hicock looked to Grand Juror Nelson and Trooper Santey. After a quick discussion, Hicock said simply, "Ten dollars and costs." The reporters wanted to know what the costs amounted to. When the court didn't seem to want to answer, the defendant, Mr. Wallace, said, "Ten dollars and twenty cents." As the reporters grumbled among themselves, Nelson said, "Boys, please don't give us too much publicity for this."

One reporter made a loud rude comment about what he thought of trial, which Hicock overheard. Giving the reporter a steely gaze, the judge warned, "Better lay off that talk or you'll be charged with contempt of court." Court was quickly dismissed and Trooper Santey escorted the people out like pushing out a flock of geese in front of him. Outside Nelson held an impromptu press conference and told the reporters that he did not have to bring the action back into court, but decided he did not want to do anything that was not on the level. They did not want to "give Southbury a black eye." It was Nelson's opinion that they had right to hold court anywhere they wanted to. He explained the reason for the secret session was to avoid publicity, but a newspapermen said by hiding away he had made matters worse.

The reporters took the opportunity to ask Nelson if the Sunday Blue Law charges against the Bund members would be dropped. Alrick Nelson answered dogmatically, "As long I am the Grand Juror, the charges will never be dropped."

33

Amos Barclay Has His Say

December 14, 1937, Tuesday

Over 200 frazzled townspeople settled into their seats at the community hall on the afternoon of Tuesday, December 14, for a special town meeting to vote on the zoning ordinances presented by the Zoning Commission. Once again reporters were in the attendance to learn exactly how the town was going to get rid of the German-American Bund. First Selectman Ed Coer opened the meeting and Rev. M. Edgar N. Lindsay was selected as the moderator once again. The call to the meeting was read by the assistant town clerk.[1]

Albert Aston, the Zoning Commission chairman, was asked to read the entire zoning code. But before he had could open up his booklet, Gregory Cassidy, Democratic town chairman, jumped up calling to be heard. "They say if you don't zone this town, the Germans will get you," he exclaimed. "It's not true. As long as the great Franklin D. Roosevelt is in the White House, he will protect us!" His outburst was greeted by boos from the Republicans, who numbered three to one over the Democrats in Southbury. Pointing toward First Selectman Coer, Cassidy claimed that the Bund was a smoke-screen used by the "Southbury Dictator" to impose zoning on the town. Gregory Cassidy sat down, satisfied that he had made his point.

The group was emotionally charged and the stress of the previous month weighed down on the townspeople. Zoning Chairman Aston read all seven pages of the zoning code. The crowd sat in silence, except for the arrival of a few late comers. When Aston had finished, there was a question about the two references to the General Statutes in the code pamphlet. Russell Hicock, a utility employee, and cousin to Judge Harold Hicock, produced copies of the General Statutes. He was allowed to read the boring legal passages about what could and could not be in town's zoning code.

The meeting was temporarily interrupted by the late arrival of former Representative Isaac C. Platt with thirty farmers from the Purchase district of town. With everyone watching, the group marched a full circle around the meeting hall, and then sought available seating. Several farmers were left standing along the walls. Platt stated loudly that they opposed the code, exclaiming that "there is no need for it."[2] Earlier during the year, Platt's farm and livelihood were taken from him through eminent domain. The state wanted his land, and the property of several other people, in order to build a state training school for the "feeble minded." Platt and his fellow farmers were protesting the state's tactics and the fact the town did nothing to stop the land grab.[3]

Amos Ewing Barclay was recognized next by the chairman. Barclay approached the platform with a book of Connecticut state statues in one hand and a copy of the zoning code in the other. Aston warned him that the Connecticut statutes were not up for debate. Barclay, who was not well known around town, stated that he was carpenter and had once been an electrical engineer. He was a tall, thin New Englander. He began by stating that the zoning code was "un-American, detrimental, un-Democratic, confiscatory, and down-right mean." The crowd disagreed loudly.

With his voice raising, Barclay stated he was against the code. "In the first place, it's contrary to the spirit of Americanism. If you want to build a building, will you have to go to Mr. Coer, pay a fee and say, 'Please can I build a building on my own land'?"

Ed Coer jumped up from his seat by the window exclaiming, "I want you to stick to the truth! There's nothing about a fee in there. Stick to the truth." The townspeople shouted their opinions and the room was close to chaos. "Order, Order!" Rev. Lindsay cried out. He effectively checked the demonstration before it became out of hand, and then nodded for Barclay to continue.

Barclay smiled. "I'm glad that point was raised. I was simply anticipating a bit there. We don't know about a fee. Not yet, at least." He went on to point out that the ordinance planned for recreation areas only situated along the Housatonic and Pomperaug Rivers. The zoning code did not make provisions for a baseball field or golf courses. "The proposed recreation district is unsuited for these sports," he said. Waving the zoning code in the air, Barclay exclaimed, "Did you notice?" He paused, waiting for everyone's full attention. "According to this ordinance, you can't bury a person in a cemetery without giving a fifteen-day notice to the zoning commission." He continued slyly, "We can let those who are in the cemetery stay; but we can't bury anyone else." Shaking his finger at the audience he said, "Don't any of you die, for heaven's sake!" Some in the crowd laughed while others protested. Robert Mitchell, the town finance chairman member simply glared at Barclay.

Mr. Lindsay struggled to regain order of the meeting, "If we can't have order I'll have to ask that the floor be cleared." When someone suggested that Barclay was taking up too much time, Lindsay explained that he was allowing Barclay to continue because he seemed to be covering the entire field of objections.

"I could go on," Barclay said amid laughter. Closing with a reference to the Bible, he said, "In the 25th chapter of Genesis, it tells the story of how Esau sold his birthright for a mess of porridge. That's what we would be doing if we passed the zoning ordinance." Mr. Barclay finished with a warning. "Southbury is selling its birthright for a mess of porridge. Be sure the pot isn't empty." He stepped off the platform to applause.

First Selectman Coer walked to the podium. "I want to thank Mr. Cassidy for the entertainment."

A puzzled Mr. Cassidy jumped up and exclaimed, "I suppose he thinks I prepared Barclay to protest, but this is only the second time in my life I have ever spoken to the man." Mr. Coer went on to praise the Zoning Commission for their work on drawing up the zoning code. "I think the commission has done a fine job and has accomplished its purpose," he said. "I believe the code will leave property and customs as we have enjoyed them for several hundred years just as they have been. I have confidence in that and shall vote for the code."

Mr. Aston rose to speak. He claimed Barclay's objections were exaggerated, but said, "I am convinced that proper zoning is not a menace to independence. The law has teeth but it wouldn't be any good unless it did. Nobody is going to get soaked by fees and no one need fear of financial injury."

George Holmes stated the zoning business had become more or less a partisan issue. "As a gas station proprietor, I could be hurt as anyone else if the commission desired to be dictatorial." However, he declared that he was "for zoning, first, last, and all the time.

Bernice Hubbell stepped out of her role as the assistant town clerk and spoke in support of zoning saying, "We can always vote for the zoning ordinance to be removed, with a petition of 20 residents."

Isaac Platt made a motion to call for the vote on the motion of accepting the zoning code. Small group discussions broke out to figure if the vote should be taken by ballot or by counting hands. The news photographers took advantage of the momentary chaos to snap a few unflattering pictures. The decision was made vote by ballot. Russell Hicock and George Tschauder were named as tellers and set up at a table. The residents stood in line alphabetically to check in and receive their slip of paper to write "yay" or "nay" on their ballot. There was a great hub-bub during the process as people figured out where they belonged in line, and then settled in for the long wait to reach the table. Persons who had been shouting angrily at one another five minutes previously were smiling and inviting each other to dinner.

The townspeople filled out that ballots and walked by a cardboard carton labeled "Fresh Ripe Tomatoes" and dropped in their vote. The counters found two blank sheets in the bottom of the box and another count was made. In the end it was assumed the voter wished to abstain. The results were announced at five o'clock. There were 142 votes in favor and ninety-one against the zoning code.

The meeting was adjourned and everyone seemed happy. In a move that surprised the officials, nobody had brought up the Bund camp during the discussion. Also, no one seemed to know or care what the Nazis were going to do with all their land in Kettletown.

Reporters crowded around the speakers to get quotes for their newspapers. Amos Barclay was asked how he felt about the camp being banned, knowing it deprived him of carpentry work ordered by the Bund. Barclay answered, "I don't give a hoot one way or the other."

Democratic Town Chairman Cassidy pointed out that only one Democrat sat on the zoning commission, although the town promised equal representation. "The code is a step from democracy to Hitlerism, the very Hitlerism we are trying to get rid of."[4]

34

Waiting to Exhale

December 1937

The reporters were gone and Southbury residents held their breath, hoping that there would finally be peace from the Bund. There was almost two weeks between the zoning code meeting and the rescheduled Blue Laws Trial on December 27.

The Blue Law trial date was pushed later in the month because of the German-American Bund's involvement in the German exposition and Christmas market. The exposition was a large occurrence, featuring many special events and 164 booths with food, handcrafts, and imported German items. Camps Nordland and Siegfried even had their own booths to advertise their recreational programs. The exposition and market were open until Christmas Eve.

Even though Wilhelm Kunze, Bund director of publicity, was also busy with the event, he had time to correspond with Rev. Lindsay. They wrote to compare notes about the philosophies of the Bund and Kunze sent informational brochures and newspapers to the pastor. Kunze invited Lindsay and his family to visit the exposition and Christmas market. He offered to give them a personal tour of the event.[1] Also in the envelope was a handmade card. On the cover it said, "*Heil*!" The inside page read "*Fröhliche Weinachten*" ("Merry Christmas") with a large swastika on the opposite page. Lindsay found this a rather unusual seasonal greeting.[2]

The young *Waterbury Republican* reporter attended the Christmas market on assignment. Bobby Abbott had been given a three-part series with his own byline. The first article covered the market and the history of the Bund. On following weeks, Bobby wrote about Camp Siegfried and Camp Nordland. He was finally a real investigative reporter.

In the middle of the month, Congress announced that Fritz Kuhn's immigration status would be investigated. They knew he had left Germany and went first to Mexico before arriving in the States. All aspects would be explored. As expected, Kuhn was unhappy with the adverse attention.

Back in Southbury, Assistant Town Clerk Bernice Hubbell reported an FBI agent stopped by the town hall. While there, he checked on the deed for Wolfgang Jung's property and borrowed newspaper clippings of the situation.[3]

Governor Wilbur Cross of Connecticut decided to make a statement about the proposed Bund camp in Southbury on December 20. The governor said he was "studying the alleged Nazi activities in Connecticut," but had taken no specific action. Congressman William Citron of Middletown had been pushing the Cross to investigate whether the Bund was directly under Hitler's control. Governor Wilbur Cross sought advice from State Attorney General Charles McLaughlin, who said that it was "not legally possible to prosecute the German-American Bund members unless they committed treasonous actions."[4]

Members of Holmes' United Americans checked on the camp site every Sunday, just in case the Bund members returned to work. The only people to appear were curiosity seekers.

35
Trial of Bund Members

December 27, 1937, Monday

The Monday afternoon trial time arrived with little fanfare. The 1 p.m. sunshine did nothing to warm the Community Hall. The decision was made it would not be worth the effort to start the furnace. Around fifty people sat on folding chairs, while huddling in their coats. Compared to the first trial for the Bund members, there were only a few reporters and photographers.

Grand Juror Alrick Nelson and attorney Basil Bass engaged in an intense conversation in the corner of the room. Nelson was still determined to follow through with the trial. Attorney Bass highly recommended dropping the case.

The defendants, Korn and Koehler, arrived and took their places in the chairs set off beside the judge's small table. Bund member Duncan Folger sat nearby to for moral support. Once again, the defendants arrived without legal counsel. Additional Bund members were in attendance were known by the townspeople, including land owner Wolfgang Jung.

Justice Hicock called the court to order. The charges were read by Grand Juror Alrick Nelson. The judge asked for a plea from Korn and Koehler, and they simply answered, "Not guilty" even though they had previously both admitted that they were working on that Sunday.[1]

In a surprise move, Nelson said, "I do not want to press the charges any further because our objective has been accomplished." He stated that the arrest stopped work at the camp site, which provided time for the zoning code to be finished and passed. This was a change of attitude from moments earlier when he emphatically said he would never consider dismissing the charges. The bond money of $75 each defendant had paid was returned, and no additional court costs were charged. "Case dismissed," proclaimed Justice Hicock, with satisfaction.

The trial had been completed within a few minutes and the defendants relaxed and engaged in friendly conversations with the Southbury residents. The campsite appeared to no longer be a threat, and the townspeople showed their friendly side, too. They genuinely wanted to know what the Bund would do with the property. Folger and Von Holt said there were no future plan in mind at the moment, but no work would be done until spring when the weather was warmer.

One of the Bund members asked Constable King if they could return to the camp on Sunday to finish some of the work. The constable advised him against it and warned that additional arrests might be made if they did. Grand Juror Nelson jumped in, making his point clear. "We won't handle them with gloves like in

Yaphank, Long Island." He indicated that he would prosecute as dogmatically as possible the next summer if the organization continued with their plans to build Camp General von Steuben.

George Holmes argued at length with Bund members Folger and Von Holt, asking various questions about the Hitler's philosophies and control of the organization. Folger told Holmes straight out that he was wrong. "You're off on the wrong foot. You have been 100 percent propagandized by the Jews."

Holmes responded by asking if real Americans could divide their loyalty between two countries. Folger protested that it was not divided loyalties, because they were for everything American, supporting the Constitution and were also in the fight against the Communists. Over all, the conversations were not in anger, even though they debating loudly. No conclusions were reached.[2]

Duncan Folger claimed he had offered to rent the community hall to have an open discussion with the town about the purposes and aims of their organization and to answer any and all questions posed by the town. He said the arrangements were already made with the first selectman. Holmes pointed out there was now the zoning code, with the Bund land in a residential and farming district. Why would the Bund bother coming back? Folger said that there had been no official discussion at the Bund headquarters, but that there were ways of "getting around" a zoning code.

Wolfgang Jung said one idea for the land was to continue working on clearing the land to build several small cottages. Fellow Bund members would be invited during the summer as guests. Jung implied that it might still be used as a campsite. Attorney Albert Aston, head of the zoning committee spoke up. "If they use that as an obvious pretext, I think the town could do something to stop it," he said. "But we had better wait and see what happens."

The hour came to an end and the Bund members left for their long drive home. Southbury citizens were confident they had done everything in their power to stop the Bund from building a camp. Holmes said he was satisfied with the outcome, even though he thought it would have been better to have a conviction on the record books.

The *Sunday Herald* offered a unique headline that summed up the whole conflict:

TO HEIL MIT HITLER.

36
Consequences

January 1938

After the end of the Blue Law Trial, Southbury was prepared for a time of reflection. The town was tired of newspaper reporters and strangers hanging around the town. They were ready to put the whole incident beyond them, but the publicity would not end yet.

The *Waterbury Republican* declared the Bund camp story as one of the top ten stories of the year of 1937. In a full-page spread of photographs, the paper included a photograph of Southbury's protest against the Nazis. The next week, the producer of a monthly newsreel company, *The March of Times*, arrived in Southbury to convince residents to take part in a reenactment of the special town meeting.[1] Her first stop was to meet with the town officials, but she failed to receive any real support. The residents were tired and were ready to move beyond the shadow of the Bund.

The planned newsreel was to be called "Inside Nazi Germany." This would be the first American movie company allowed inside of Nazi Germany with a free pass to film anything—under the guidance of the Nazi hosts, of course. Scenes filmed included Nazi work projects, storm troopers, children marching, a Jewish park bench, and several other forbidden places. The movie producer convinced *Bundesführer* Fritz Kuhn to allow them an interview in the Bund headquarters. However, they did not tell him the real purpose of the movie was to expose the Bund as Nazis.

Going directly to the Southbury townspeople, the movie company came up with an offer. Each person who would appear for the filming would receive $2. When the producer still did not find enough extras, the price was raised to $4—about a week's wage for some residents—and this tactic attracted a sufficient number of recruits to play the townspeople re-enacting the special meeting. George Holmes and Jennie Hinman were the only ones with a speaking role. The town decided to support the film, because it might help someone else or another location in a similar circumstance.[2]

Warner Theaters across the nation decided to ban the movie at the beginning. They thought that the pictures depicted a positive side of Nazi Germany. Upon further examination, and listening closely to the anti-Nazi narrative in the film, the ban was lifted. A special showing of the "Nazis in Germany" was set up for Fritz Kuhn, and the film-makers added hidden microphones to the room to catch his reaction. Kuhn's response was swift and vehement. In his heavy German accent, he exclaimed, "If Hitler sees the film, I will be ruint. Ruint! Ruint![3]

The newsreel gave courage to others to speak out against the Bund and similar organizations. Even though the Bund attempted to establish other camps throughout America, there was great resistance and pushback from the towns. Many who had feared the Bund now took a firm stand against them. The Bund found opposition at every turn. Southbury had set an example to the nation.

With Southbury passing a zoning code, many surrounding towns decided to follow their lead. The goal was to make sure the Bund did not find a home in Connecticut. For many years afterwards, Southbury officials received requests for copies of their zoning code booklet and advice about developing a zoning commission in their own town.

Southbury residents were proud of themselves for heeding Rev. Lindsay's advice. He had said, "...we are not against men, but against movements that hurt men." Stopping the German-American Bund from settling in Southbury, kept the evil philosophies out of the town and protected the children from Nazi influence.

America's ambassador to Germany until December 1937, William Dodd, appeared on the Anti-Nazi Honor Roll. He was commended for his stand against the Nazis, which caused him to be removed from Germany. Southbury also received the highest praise that could possibly be extended to a Yankee community when the Anti-Nazi Honor Roll recognized Southbury: "For setting an example of stubborn local opposition to the advance of the Nazi training camps in America."[4]

EPILOGUE:

Not the End

Southbury returned to their normal routines and the fears of the Nazi invasion lessened with each day. However, the story did not end after the zoning meeting or the trial. The German-American Bund continued to claim that they would return to build on the property. The Bund eastern organizer was determined the town should not get too comfortable.

In March 1938, Carl Nicolay issued a statement saying that the Bund would be returning to Southbury as soon as the ground thawed. He claimed the Sunday work schedule was being drawn up by the developing Bund units in New York and Stamford, Connecticut, and they had already ordered supplies. Nicolay said there were ways to work around the zoning codes.

Meanwhile, the United Americans' members continued to patrol the campsite area. Sometimes they found picnickers, but did not see any Bund members.

Citizens formed a group called the New Haven Anti-Nazi League to fight against the establishment of the Bund Unit in their town. Professor Robert L. Calhoun, of the Yale Divinity School, was elected as the chairman. Calhoun had an answer to the Bund's claims they were "one-hundred percent American." He said: "This seems a little like calling darkness one-hundred percent daylight." Calhoun also said that the Bund's leadership principle "of unquestioning obedience and compulsory uniformity" was totally in opposition to American democracy."[1]

Carl Nicolay released a statement in May saying the Bund had no intention of giving up on their plans for Camp General von Steuben. A steering committee of members from the Westchester County and the Connecticut districts would take charge of the project. When asked again about the zoning laws in Southbury, Nicolay said, "That will be fixed." The constables kept an eye on the property during the summer, but noting there were no activities at the campsite.[2]

A September announcement was released several months later by Gustave Buckel, the newly appointed Bund leader for the state of Connecticut. He said the land would be turned into a model German community. Parcels of land would be sold to the Bund members, who would be allowed to build their own homes. The community would have their own church and school right in the middle of the camp site.[3]

When asked about this proposal, George Holmes stated there might not be anything the town could do about it. The chairman of the zoning commission reported that if the Bund followed the zoning regulations, the German housing development would have to be allowed.

But within the same month, Buckel made another statement saying, "the sentiments against the Bund in Southbury has changed." Holmes answered, "Perhaps the sentiments *have* changed. We are more determined than ever to the keep the Nazis out."

Apparently, Buckel did not talk with Duncan Folger, head of the Westchester unit, who had been involved in the Southbury project from the beginning. Folger sent out his own press release to say that the Bund property for Camp von Steuben would be sold. The reason was because it was not in the middle of the State, making it difficult for all of the planned Connecticut groups to reach the camp. He also stated that the engineers had decided that the land was too steep for handling the expected large weekend crowds with complete safety.

Gustave Buckel ended up having problems working for the Bund and did not last long as the leader. He was arrested for embezzling funds from the organization and released from his position.

In the same year, Pulitzer Prize winning playwright, Elmer Rice, wrote *American Landscape: A Play in Three Acts* loosely based on the Southbury and the old families like the Hinmans. His story told of old family in a small town, called Dalesford, Connecticut. The play follows the efforts of the younger members of the family trying to prevent their father from selling the family estate to the Bund. Rice liked to lace his plays with political messages, including the dangers of fascism. American Landscape was the first play to attack the evil of Nazism.[4]

The next year, 1939, Southbury real estate agent and constable, John King, received an offer for the Bund property. Sheriff J. Edward Slavin of Bridgeport, Connecticut, was looking for a place to build a camp for the "First Offenders Club." This was an organization aimed at keeping children from breaking the law and becoming first offenders. Slavin's goals were to get the children away from the big cities and into a summer camp to enjoy the fresh air. His reasons were very similar to the Bund's stated purpose in making their recreational camps.[5]

Fritz Kuhn immediately said that the Bund would not sell their property to the Sheriff Slavin because he only offered $1,000 for the land.

A surprise news story was published in May 1940 reporting the German-American Bund had surveyors working on the grounds of the camp site. A reliable source believed that Bund was looking for a new regional headquarters for the Eastern division. The proposed plans included an auditorium to hold 1,000 people. Even though the zoning code prohibited a camp on the land, the Bund officials believed an auditorium would be allowed. They were also expected to apply for a liquor license and were confident it would be granted in Connecticut.[6] Either the reliable source had incorrect information or the Bund decided the plan was not feasible.

Within a matter of months, former Stamford Bund leader George Munk purchased the land from Wolfgang Jung. Munk owned a carpentry business and harvested lumber from the property as needed. At this time, the road signs directing the way to Camp von Steuben were removed.

The town went back to an uneasy calmness. Even though it appeared the Bund would not return, the town still feared Bund repercussions. During World War II, lookouts were set up on various hillsides in Southbury, watching for any type of enemy airplanes. Mrs. Henry McCarthy said, "We were always afraid that if Hitler sent his bombers to America, they would come to Southbury first, because we kicked the Nazis out."[7]

This story was temporarily lost in history with only occasional mentions. One day the town clerk, Joyce Hornbecker, found the original typed copies of the zoning code and told the story to a *Waterbury Republican-American* reporter, who wrote a feature on the story. Interest in the time the Nazis came to Southbury blossomed. In 2012, the Southbury Historical Society commissioned film-maker Scott Sniffen to make a movie to document the incident.

Since the release of the movie, *Home of the Brave, When Southbury Said "No" to the Nazis*, thousands of people have learned about the strength of Southbury's residents, and their example standing against a bully and facing evil head on. Copies of the movie can be found in museums all around the country and even overseas. The United States Holocaust Memorial Museum in Washington, D.C., currently have a display with Southbury and Rev. M.E.N. Lindsay artifacts.

The bravery of the small town to stand against the Nazis is relevant to all generations. Southbury residents took the time to listen to others and their conflicting points of views during the special town meetings. While they did not always agree with each other's politics, they looked past their differences to work together to solve a problem.

APPENDIX I

What Happened To?

Southbury Heroes

George Holmes led the United Americans until it naturally dissolved at the beginning of World War II. His little shop next to his gas pump supplied newspapers and magazines, along with a limited supply of groceries and penny candy. He enjoyed interacting with the students from the White Oak Schoolhouse when they stopped by to get snacks on their way home from school.

James Edward Coer was the town's first selectman from 1933 to 1947. In a short memoir, *50 Years of Southbury*, he wrote about his time in office including when the Bund was in town. In 1962, he joined forces with the former chairman of the Democratic Town Committee, Gregory F. Cassidy to attempt to overturn the zoning code. They both felt that the current zoning commission had too much power.

Neil Agnew, the vice president of Paramount Pictures, and his wife, Arlene Francis, lived part-time in Southbury until their divorce in 1945. Agnew remarried in Southbury. He sold his property to the comedian Ed Sullivan in 1953.

Reverend M. E. N. Lindsay stayed at the South Britain Congregational Church from 1928 to 1941. He moved his family back to Virginia to work at the Lynchburg College during the war. He served as a pastor in Tazewell, Virginia, for twenty years before retiring. Lindsay continued to use his typewriter as a tool to educate the public and to fight for freedom.

Reverend Felix Manley left Southbury just two years later. In 1939, he was called to South Hadley, Massachusetts where he served for five years. He went on to preach in Hawaii and California.

C. Robert Abbott worked his way up from rookie reporter to a full reporter and eventually an editor at the *Waterbury Republican* American. He was a resident of Southbury for many years and retired in Maine.

Jennie Hinman moved her residency permanently to Southbury just a few years before the Bund arrived. She actively served the community until her death in 1945.

David S. Joselowitz served as a constable in Southbury for over twenty years. His family was the only Jewish family residing in town during the 1930s.

The Bundist

Fritz Kuhn, leader of the Bund, did not handle rejection well. He pushed harder for Bund Units to build youth camps. Following Southbury's lead, many residents protested having a camp in their neighborhood. Kuhn became open in his Antisemitic views. With the FBI following his every move, it was not long before he was arrested for taking money from the Bund accounts. He spent time in Sing Sing during the war, and was sent to Dachau camp in Germany. The officials had hoped to have Kuhn testify in the Nuremburg trials, but he escaped from Dachau. He took a job in a small town, where he stayed the rest of his life.

Gerhard Wilhelm Kunze became the leader of the Bund after Kuhn was arrested in 1939, but was not accepted well in the Bund community. He was charged with inciting racial hatred in New Jersey and was sentenced to fourteen months in prison. The charges were dropped on appeal. Kunze fled to Mexico and planned to buy a boat to go to Germany. The FBI found him and Kunze was arrested and sent to Hartford, Connecticut, to stand trial on a separate charge of conspiracy to violate the Espionage Act. He pleaded guilty and was sentenced to fifteen years in prison.

Carl Nicolay had been a frequent visitor to Camp General von Steuben in Southbury. He also served as the liaison between the Bund and the Connecticut newspapers. Along with seven other Bund officials, he was to be arrested on charges of obtaining their American citizenship fraudulently. However, Nicolay escaped to Germany where he was said to join Hitler's forces. After the war, the American soldiers arrested Nicolay on charges of treason against the USA. He never returned to America to stand trial.

Wolfgang T. Jung, owner of the 178 acres in Southbury, was a driving force and sustaining member in the Stamford Bund until Hitler declared war on American. He was quickly picked up by the FBI and taken to a detention center on charges of espionage. Even though he was scheduled to be sent back to Germany, he was allowed to stay in America near his family during the war. After the war, his architect business was very successful, designing and building many public schools and offices. He sold the Southbury property to George Munk, the former leader of the Stamford Bund.

George Munk, owner of the General Woodworking Company in Stamford, Connecticut, harvested trees from the property for his carpentry business. He left the Bund before purchasing the land. When approached by reporters, he was unwilling to discuss the subject. "That was a sale and that is all," was his reluctant statement. He asked for the reporters to not bother him again. George Munk held onto the old Bund property until 1976, when he started to sell parcels of land to developers for housing. He sold his last section in 1980. The houses on Sleepy Hill Road and many along the Bullet Hill Road are on the old Bund land.

Adolf Hitler became a powerful and evil force in the world. He did not understand why his philosophies were not accepted in America. Hitler remarked: "If you transplant a German to Kiev, he remains a perfect German. But transplant him to Miami, and you make a degenerate out of him—in other words, an American."

APPENDIX II

Reverend M. E. N. Sermon to South Britain Congregational Church

NAZISM—AN ANTI-CHRISTIAN MENACE.

I propose to show that the Bible describes for us the nature of an anti-Christ. I propose to demonstrate that the Nazi movement in practice fulfills the designation. I shall argue that the connection between the German-American Bund is such as to warrant the claim that it is a Nazi movement. I shall remind you that this same Bund proposes to establish within our own town a camp similar to those established elsewhere, which are but a replica of those established in Germany by Hitler in the early days of the Nazi movement. And finally, I shall offer several suggestions as to what might be done to relieve us of this insidious menace.

What is an anti-Christ?

Any person, or any body or persons whose principles, policies or practices deny the historical Christ, the same is an anti-Christ. Any person or body of persons who depart from that which is taught in the doctrine of Christ is an anti-Christ. This is a fair statement, readily deduced from our text, which I now read from the second letter of John, verses seven and nine a. "For many deceivers are entered into the world, who confess not that Jesus Christ is come in the flesh. This is a deceiver and an anti-Christ...whosoever transgresseth and abideth not in the doctrine of Christ, hath not God."

History numbers many appearances of deceivers who fit the above measure. Hence, we need not be greatly surprised if there appear in our day and time those who fit the scriptural description of the anti-Christ. But while we are not surprised at their appearance, we must be ready to recognize and denounce such as may be so numbered. We are forced, therefore, to examine the Nazi movement, and as we examine it, to weigh it in the light of our text. Is the Nazi movement anti-Christ?

Nazism.

In Hitler's *Mein Kampf*, we find he takes the position that, "We shall have no strange Gods." He is laying down the policies that his movement will tolerate no split loyalties. One may not serve both God and Mammon. Indeed, as we shall learn, he might have said, ye may not serve God!

As Nazism moved from the stage of the hypothetical to that of the practical government, Hitler appointed Rosenburg with jurisdiction in matters of education, creeds and cults. The plan was to absorb Christianity into the German cultus. This minister of education shows the anti-Christ color of the Nazi movement in his book, THE MYTH OF THE THIRTEENTH CENTURY, where he gives a picture of the Nordi Christ, a warrior, tall, lean, handsome, strong, and above all, light-haired. The novelist, F.A.S. Noerr, in his work, THE ENTRANCE OF OUR GOOD LADY, tells how Christianity, as a myth fused with Teutonic legends in the countries north of the Alps, thus denying the validity of the historical Christ. Now when we remember that nothing is permitted in Germany but that which has the stamp of official approval, we are forced to conclude that the Government fosters an anti-Christ propaganda.

In addition to the direct denial or the Historical Christ, we observe that Nazism fails also to walk in the doctrine of the Christ. The very practice of the Nazi government in its persecution of the Jews alone condemns it at this point. The conceited claim of Germanic superiority, philosophically set forth by that little extrovert, Nitzsche, and enthusiastically adopted by the ego-centric Hitler, can hardly be considered a gesture of Christian brotherhood.

The resurrection of the pagan Gods under the inspiration of General von Ludendorff, who, we remember, wears a skull on his military hat, is more anti-Christ than the atheistic Communists, who at least accept a workable law in operation in the world, albeit, they do not give God the credit for originating the law.

And what shall we say of the persecution of the church, Protestant and Roman Catholic, with the view of having the swastika triumph over the Cross? What shall we say when a national hero, war commander of the *U-73*, and later of the more famous *U-115* and the *U-67*, who, at the close of the war, became a minister, now suffers imprisonment for daring to insist that "he ought to obey God rather than Man." He it was, Niemoeller, who, because his people feared the police, celebrated Holy Communion in his own church with nobody present except three young secret service men "who have to inform upon the community of Jesus in their praying, in their singing and their teaching; young men who were certainly baptized in the name of Jesus who certainly have pledged their faith to the Savior, who are now laying traps for his flock."

And what shall we say when a young Protestant boy from Stuttgart was ejected from a STRENGTH THROUGH JOY camp, one similar to that now proposed in Southbury, for destructive tendencies, who, when his ex-pugilist platoon leader called on him in class, "Wilhelm, what is Christianity?" replied, "Christianity is, Christianity was, a philosophy of life." The leader's fist came down with a crash;

he struck him again and again, before giving his own definition of unprintable obscenity. "Say it after me, you idiot! Chris...Christiani...No I won't." You may imagine the rest.

Yes, my friends, Nazism will brook no rival. It makes a totalitarian claim. Rosenburg, speaking on June 6th or this year, defined the scope of the state as follows: "National Socialism has not appealed to only a part of the German man or woman, but to the whole man and the whole woman, and therefore Germans accept it wholly." It not only denies Christ. It persecutes His Church, seeking to obliterate His doctrine. It is therefore anti-Christ.

Is the German-American Bund Nazi?

We are now informed by the *Waterbury American* for November 15th, that Carl Nicolay, the eastern division organizer of the Bund, "recently spent a year in Germany lecturing on the Bund's activities here." We might rest assured he would not be tolerated that long if he were extolling the virtues of American democracy. No, to be heard, indeed to be allowed to lecture at all, he must have a contribution to make to Nazism. He must show how these camps are favorable to Nazi views, if not indeed, actively espousing the Nazi cause.

Add to this the stated Nazi attempt to retain the loyalty of the people of German blood in other countries, and add also, the unintended findings of Edward Windsor when he unfortunately got into the wrong building as he was presumably studying housing recently in Germany, and observed the ado made over the Bund camps in America, and we may conclude that the German-America Bund is indeed and in truth, an arm of the Nazi program. And if the body be anti-Christ, what of the arm?

The Camp in Southbury.

May I call your attention to the fact that the proposed camp in Southbury is to be, according to the information given the reporter of the *Waterbury Republican*, one of the country's largest; that it apparently will be modeled after those now located at Yaphank L.I. and Andover N.J. You will perhaps recall the recent military demonstration at one of these camps, with the attending censure and alarm. Judging from the camps already established, one is reminded of the early camps of the Nazi movement in Germany, where the effort was first to interest youth, later to drill the youth, and still later, served as barracks for storm troopers. What are we to assume will be the future of this camp, if allowed to go unchallenged? Incidentally, it is interesting to note that the plan as stated, is to use Sundays to clear the ground for the camp—a splendid Christian gesture.

In the light of what I have said, I maintain these camps are highly undesirable, because first, the whole movement is un-Christian; as I have already shown; second, it is un-American, for it proposed to foster the philosophy of a foreign government;

and third, it is pro-Nazi, by the admission of its own leaders, who according to Mr. Jung, "want to establish a better understanding between the citizens of this country and Germany, even though the two governments are different in character. "We want," he says, "the two countries to be on friendly terms with each other with no secrets or squabbles," for, "if we are open about what is going on, there will be no war or disputes." Just how this camp is to accomplish the work of the Department of State, and the Foreign Office of Germany, I do not readily see, assuming of course, that we are going to have no secrets each from the other.

What May be Done About It?

We are not helpless in this matter, thank God! There are several thing we may do. We may urge that all aliens connected with this move, if any, be returned as undesirable. Our representatives in Congress may be appealed to on this point. Also, we may urge them to devise such legislation as may be needed to cope with such movements when they show a semi-military character. Again we may inquire of the immigration courts if a naturalized American has not violated his oath of citizenship when he indulges in the pastime of fostering the view of a foreign potentate or country, loyalty to which he had forever forsworn. If he has violated his oath, he thereby forfeits his citizenship rights. These things we may do, as a defense against the whole movement, by writing our representatives in Congress as well as the Governor of our state, which I have already done.

Locally, we may pass a zoning regulation, which may result in refusing permission to build, if such a building would prove undesirable to the community as a whole.

Let us therefore take council together my friends, and lend our efforts to the cause of the Righteousness of Christ, beginning with our community, and extending to the uttermost parts of the world.

APPENDIX III

Resolution Presented to Mass Meeting by George Holmes

"We the people of Southbury, Connecticut, citizens of the United States of America, in mass meeting assembled, after calm and careful deliberation, find that:

"Whereas, there has recently been purchased a tract of land within our township for the avowed purpose of using same for a recreation and concentration camp of Nazi American youths, and,

"Whereas, from documentary evidence and other good and sufficient reasons we believe these camps to be governed and directed by a foreign government inimical to our continuance as a Democracy, and,

"Whereas, in furtherance of their designs against our national unity and sovereignty the agents of this foreign government are teaching these youths the philosophy of Naziism, drilling them in Nazi German military tactics with the expressed purpose of dominating our national affairs to the profit of Naziism and a democracy, and,

"Whereas, these activities can only be construed as unfriendly acts of conspiracy and invasion:

"Therefore, be it resolved that we, citizens of Southbury, secure in the liberties and privileges bequeathed us by our fathers, and sincerely determined to hand this precious heritage to our children, do, herby petition and pray the President of the United States, the Senate, the representatives in Congress and the governor of our state, to employ the power vested in them to abate, dispel, and destroy this menace to our constituted government.

"In witness of the sincerity of our purpose and our determination to protect our government against the insidious attack of alien forces, we hereby attach our signatures this 23rd day of November, 1937.

Endnotes

Chapter 1

1 Clark, H., *Saga of Pomperaug Plantation* (Southbury Tercentennial Committee: Southbury, 1973).
2 Town Records—Records of Special Town Meeting held on February 15, 1819.
3 Lakeside Ads and sign about "Christian Community."
4 "Forgotten Shame: Ku Klux Klan No Stranger To CT," *Hartford Courant*, November 17, 2016.
5 *50 Years of Southbury*, James Edward Coer, 1962, Southbury Historical Society Bund Collection.
6 "Barleycorn's Grave Gives Up Its Liquor," *The Wichita Eagle*, May 8, 1928.
7 "Selectman Fined in Gambling Case," *New Britain Herald*, December 18, 1930.
8 *Story of Old Hundred*, written by Nellie Brown—Southbury Historical Society Old Hundred Collection.

Chapter 2

1 "New Popular Idol Rises in Bavaria," *The New York Times*, November 21, 1922.
2 Kohler, Wilhelm, *Die Nationale Revolution in Deutschland. Ein Gedenkbuch in Bildern,* (Minden: Druck und Verlag von Wilhelm Kohler, 1933).
3 "Germany Is Slipping Into Communism, Says Hitler," Von Wiegar, Karl H., *The San Francisco Examiner*, January 5, 1930.
4 "Poor Can Now Hear Hitler," *Hartford Courant*, December 29, 1937.
5 "Nazis Must Eat Stew," *Hammond Times*, Hammond, Indiana, December 10, 1937.

Chapter 3

1 *Court transcript with Fritz Grissibl*, Investigation of Un-American Propaganda.

Chapter 4

1 *American Churches to Hitler*; Booklet by American Federal Council of Churches, June 4, 1937; Southbury Historical Society, Bund Collection.
2 *South Britain Parish Program of Activity–1929,* by Rev. Lindsay. Report to Yale Divinity School.

Chapter 5

1 *Made In America: Americans in Support of the Nazi Cause*, Ronald H. Bailey, April 2014 issue of World War II.
2 *United States v. Bregler et al*, US District court for the Eastern District of New York, (55 F Supp. 837 1944).
3 Letter from Carl Nicolay in Germany to his replacement, Hoffman in New York. From the FBI Files, German-American Bund.
4 *Ibid.*

Chapter 6

1 *Nordland*, Southbury Historical Society Original Document, a brochure 1937.
2 "Nazi Camps Probe Sought," *Daily News*, New York, New York, August 1, 1937.
3 "Nazis charged With Making '4-H' Propaganda Drive on U.S.," *Evening Star*, Washington, D.C., September 10, 1937.

Chapter 7

1 Various newspapers reports on November 15, 1937.
2 "Nazi Bund Spawned Southbury Zoning," *Danbury News Times*, November 1978.
3 "When Southbury Foiled Hitler," *Voices*, July 12, 1977.
4 "Aged Southbury Man Shot In Hold Up," *Hartford Courant*, November 7, 1937.
5 Based on oral history. There appears to be no written record of who was in the car. C. Robert Abbot wrote a report in 1952 saying that Fritz Kuhn came to town. However, there were numerous errors in his account so many years later.

Chapter 8

1 Letter from Wolfgang Jung to Southbury Town Clerk, September 25, 1937; Southbury Historical Society Bund Files.
2 Town Records, Deed of Sale, October 27, 1937, Town Clerk, Town Hall, Southbury.
3 *50 Years of Southbury*, James Edward Coer, 1962, Southbury Historical Society Bund Collection.

Chapter 9

1 "Nation's Largest Pro-Nazi Camp Started in Southbury by German-American Bund," *Waterbury Republican*, November 15, 1937.
2 Land Records for Neil Agnew Property, Town Clerk's Office, Southbury Town Hall.
3 *Deutscher Weckruf und Beobachter*, the regional Bund newspaper. December 2, 1937.

Chapter 10

1 "Nation's Largest Pro-Nazi Camp Started in Southbury by German-American Bund," *Waterbury Republican*, November 15, 1937.
2 "Southbury Folk Surprised, but Silent," *Bridgeport Post*, November 16, 1937.
3 *50 Years of Southbury*, James Edward Coer, 1962.

Chapter 11

1 "Legion Opposes Formation of Nazi Bridgeport Unit," *Hartford Courant*, November 16, 1937.

2 Connecticut State Library, Archives Room, Wilbur Cross Papers, 1937–1938, Box # 409, Nazi Camp-Southbury Folder.

Chapter 12

1 Call to Meeting, November 17, 1937, original document. Southbury Historical Society Bund collection.

Chapter 13

1 "A Taxpayer and a Mother," Letter to the Editor, *Waterbury Republican* November 18, 1937.
2 Kettletowners Warning to Southbury, original document, Southbury Historical Society Bund Collection.
3 "George Holmes," Letter to the Editor, *Waterbury Republican*, November 18, 1937.
4 "Queer Friendship Tactics, Editorial," *Waterbury Republican*, November 18, 1937.

Chapter 14

1 Reverend Lindsay's correspondence, November 18, 1937—copies of letters in the South Britain Congregational Church Archives and in the Southbury Historical Society Bund Collection.

Chapter 15

1 "Bund Fighting for America," *New Haven* Register, November 21, 1937.
2 Carl Nicolay quoted in the *Deutscher Weckruf und Beobachter*, the regional Bund newspaper, December 2, 1937.

Chapter 16

1 "Hitler Enlists the Germans Everywhere," Tolischus, Otto D., *The New York Times* Sunday Magazine, November 21, 1937.
2 Carl Nicolay, Letter to the Editor, *Waterbury Republican*, November 21, 1937.
3 "George Holmes Claims Bund is Illegal Group," *Waterbury Republican*, November 21, 1937.

Chapter 17

1 Eyewitness account, Conversation with Carol Lindsay Hagy, via phone with Melinda Elliott and Kimberly Neuenschwander, 2019.
2 *Sermon by Rev. Lindsay*; November 21, 1937, copy in Southbury Historical Society Bund Collection.
3 *Felix Manley's letter to Roscoe Nelson of The Advance Magazine*; December 13, 1937, Southbury Historical Society Bund Collection.
4 "Warner Speaks at Meeting of Bible Students;" unknown newspaper clipping, *c.* November 1937, SHS Bund Files.
5 Editorial in *Jewish Ledger*, November 20, 1937.
6 *Thanksgiving Sermon*, November 24, 1937, American Jewish Archives, Cincinnati, Ohio, Abraham Feldman Collection.
7 "Feldman Asks Welcome To Nazi Camp Be Cool," *Hartford Courant*, November 20, 1937.

Chapter 18

1 Numerous newspapers reports.
2 Minutes of Special Meeting, Town Clerk, Southbury Town Hall.
3 Eyewitness account, Hal V. Champoli at Bullet Hill School, October 25, 2019. Hal attended the meeting with his parents and sister. The parents wanted the children to see the town in action.
4 Minutes of Special Meeting, Town Clerk, Southbury Town Hall.
5 *Ibid.*

Chapter 19

1 Resolution by George Holmes, Connecticut State Library, Archives Room, Wilbur Cross Papers, 1937-1938, Box # 409, Nazi Camp-Southbury Folder.

Chapter 20

1 *America Speaks*, The Record, (Hackensack, New Jersey, November 22, 1937).
2 Fritz Kuhn was quoted in the December 2, 1937 edition of the *Deutscher Weckruf und Beobachter*, the regional Bund newspaper. "Simultaneous attacks came from a Jewish judge in New Jersey and from a tiny community in Connecticut and elsewhere..." Carol Hagy Collection, Lindsay Scrapbook, Southbury Historical Society.
3 Online Article*: Vonsiatsky Espionage,* www.fbi.gov/history/famous-cases/vonsiatsky-espionage.

Chapter 21

1 Connecticut State Library, Archives Room, Wilbur Cross Papers, 1937–1938, Box # 409, Nazi Camp-Southbury Folder.

Chapter 22

1 "Oath To Hitler," *Waterbury Republican*, November 28, 1937.
2 McCall, M., *Kingdom Come* (Steeger, 1937).
3 *Foreign Political Movements in the United States*. Hanighen, Frank C., (Foreign Affairs, periodical, October 1, 1937).
4 *Orders G-Men To Scan Nazi Camps in U.S.,* (Daily News, New York, New York, August 19, 1937).

Chapter 23

1 Based on later correspondence between Wilhelm Kunze and Rev. Lindsay. Letters are owned by the Southbury Historical Society.
2 *Felix Manley's letter to Roscoe Nelson of The Advance Magazine*; December 13, 1937, Southbury Historical Society Bund Collection.

Chapter 24

1 "Southburians Called to Zone Hearing December 14," *Waterbury Republican*, November 29, 1937.

Chapter 25

1 Letter from *Herr* Schmidt to Rev. Lindsay, confessing he was really Kurt Saher, United States Holocaust Memorial Museum, Rev. M. E. N. Lindsay Papers (also available online at ushmm.org).
2 German-American Bund Application, original document, Southbury Historical Society Bund Collection.
3 Eyewitness account—George Harrison, during visit to Old Town Hall Museum, March 23, 2019.
4 Eyewitness account—Gladys Bartlett, daughter of Judge Harold Hicock. Notations and personal experiences added to Dorothy Schling's report *circa* 1987: *The Expulsion of the German-American Bund From Southbury, Connecticut,* Southbury Historical Society Bund Collection.
5 *Retelling of the story by Carol Lindsay Hagy,* via phone with Melinda Elliott and Kimberly Neuenschwander, 2019.
6 *50 Years of Southbury*, James Edward Coer, 1962, Southbury Historical Society Bund Collection.
7 "Postcard from One Hundred Percent Americans to Rev. Lindsay," original document, Southbury Historical Society Bund Collection.

Chapter 26

1 Arrest Warrants, original documents, Southbury Historical Society Bund Collection.
2 Newspaper Reporters at the Bund camp, included *Waterbury Republican* and *Bridgeport Telegram.*
3 Eyewitness account—Gladys Bartlett, daughter of Judge Harold Hicock. Notations and personal experiences added to Dorothy Schling's report *circa* 1987: *The Expulsion of the German-American Bund From Southbury, Connecticut,* Southbury Historical Society Bund Collection.

Chapter 27

1 Letter from Gladys Bartlett to Ken Burns, August 2008, Southbury Historical Society.
2 Interactions from eyewitness accounts and newspaper articles.
3 Connecticut State Library, Archives Room, Box 393, Car repair exceptions: Automobiles, Statute Forbidding Repair and Sale on Sundays.

Chapter 28

1 "Patriotic Group Forms in Southbury," *Hartford Courant*, December 11, 1937.
2 "Heils Are Absent," *The New York Times*, July 26, 1937.
3 "Topic of the The Times," *The New York Times*, December 6, 1937.
4 *Felix Manley's letter to Roscoe Nelson of The Advance Magazine*; December 13, 1937, Southbury Historical Society Bund Collection.
5 "Sworn to Duty," *Waterbury Republican*, December 13, 1937.
6 Conversation with Lorraine Cable, granddaughter of Alrick Nelson, October 2020.

Chapter 29

1 "Southbury's Zoning Code Bars Use Of Bund Camp For Recreational Or Drills," *Waterbury Republican*, December 8, 1937.
2 *Zoning Regulations for Town of Southbury Connecticut, 1937*, booklet, Southbury Zoning Commission, December 1937. Copy available at the Southbury Historical Society.

Chapter 30

1 "Anti-Bund Chief Ex-Klan Leader," *The Waterbury Democrat*, December 9, 1937.
2 50 Years of Southbury.
3 "Anti-Bund Chief Ex-Klan Leader," *The Waterbury Democrat*, December 9, 1937.

Chapter 31

1 Incident was gleaned from numerous newspapers and oral histories.
2 "Southbury Red Hot Over Bund Case but Justice Hall's Cold," *Waterbury American*, December 12, 1937.
3 *Waterbury Republican* photograph, December 12, 1937.
4 Pathé Newsreel.

Chapter 32

1 *Arrest Warrant for Edward Wallace, December 10, 1937*, original document, Southbury Historical Society Bund Collection.

Chapter 33

1 Minutes to Town Meeting of December 14, 1937, Town Clerk's Office, Southbury Town Hall.
2 "A Stink Bomb Burst During 'The Battle of Southbury';" *Sunday Herald*, December 20, 1937.
3 Deed for property of Isaac Platt, Land Records, Town Clerk's Office, Southbury Town Hall.
4 Numerous newspaper reports.

Chapter 34

1 Handwritten Letter from Wilhelm Kunze to Rev. Lindsay, December 20, 1937. United States Holocaust Memorial Museum.
2 Christmas Card from Wilhelm Kunze to Rev. Lindsay. Southbury Historical Society, Carol Hagy Collection, Rev. Lindsay Scrapbook.
3 "Bund Activity is Investigated by Federal Men," *Waterbury Republican*, December 16, 1937.
4 "Governor Cross is Studying Bund," *Waterbury Democrat*, December 20, 1937.

Chapter 35

1 Court records written on arrest warrants. Original documents, Southbury Historical Society Bund Collection.
2 Reports in various newspapers.

Chapter 36

1 "Southbury May Get Into Movie," *Waterbury Republican*, January 4, 1938.
2 Felding, Raymond, *General Information From The March of Time 1935–1951* (New York, Oxford University Press, 1978).
3 *Anti-Nazis Listed in "Nation" Honor Roll of 31*, Jewish Telegraphic Agency, January 5, 1938.

Epilogue

1 "Sees New Freedom For Germany When Fascism is Halted," *Hartford Courant*, April 26, 1938.
2 "Bund to Push Camp Project at Southbury," *Waterbury Republican*, May 31, 1938.
3 "Southbury sounds 'Call to Arms' As Bund Plans 'Model Community,'" *Stamford Daily Advocate*, September 14, 1938.
4 Rice, Elmer, *American Landscape: A Play in Three Acts*, (Coward-McCann, Incorporated, 1939).
5 "Offers Bund Price On Southbury Land," *Stamford Daily Advocate*, March 10, 1939.
6 "Land to Become Bund Eastern Headquarters," *The Berkshire Eagle*, Pittsfield, MA, May 28, 1940.
7 "Nazi Bund Spawned Southbury Zoning," *Danbury News Times*, November 1978.

Bibliography

Bell, L., *In Hitler's Shadow: The Anatomy of American Nazism* (Kennikat: London, 1973)

Bernstein, A., *Swastika Nation* (St. Martin's: New York, 2013)

Canedy, S., *America's Nazis: A Democratic Dilemma (Markgraf Publication Groups, 1990)*

Clark, H., *Saga of Pomperaug Plantation* (Southbury Tercentennial Committee: Southbury, 1973)

Diamond, S., *The Nazi Movement in the United States, 1924-1941* (Cornell: Ithaca, 1974)

Doherty, T., *Hollywood and Hitler 1933-1939* (Columbia: New York, 2013)

Duffy, J., *Target America: Hitler's Plan to Attack the United States* (Lyons: Guilford, 2004)

Fischer, J., *Nazi Germany: A New History* (Continuum: New York, 1995)

Frye, A., *Nazi Germany and the American Hemisphere 1933-1941* (Yale: New Haven/ London, 1967)

Greene, Daniel and Phillips, Edward, *Americans and the Holocaust*, (Rutgers University Press: New Jersey, 2022)

Higham, C., *American Swastika* (Doubleday: New York, 1985)

McCall, M., *Kingdom Come* (Steeger, 1937)

Miller, M., *Wunderlich's Salute* (Malamud-Rose: Smithtown, 1983)

Nagorski, A., *HitlerLand: American Eyewitnesses to the Nazi Rise to Power* (Schuster: New York, 2012)

O'Connor, R., *The German-American: An Informal History (Little Brown & Company, 1968)*

Pateman, C., *Beheaded by Hitler: Cruelty of the Nazis, Civilian Executions, and Judicial terror 1933-1945* (Fonthill: UK, 2014)

Rice, E., *American Landscape: A Play in Three Acts (*Coward-McCann, Inc., 1939

Riess, C., *Total Espionage, Germany's Information and disinformation Apparatus 1932-1941 (Fonthill Media LLC, 2016)*

Ross, S., *Hitler in Los Angeles: How Jews foiled Nazi Plots Against Hollywood and America,* (Bloomsbury USA, 2017)

Stowe, L., *Nazi Means War* (Whittlesey: New York, 1934)

Southbury History

Cothren, William, *History of Ancient Woodbury, Connecticut* (William Cothren, 1872)
Elliott, Melinda K., *Southbury History Through Time: Remnants of our Past* (Fonthill Media 2019)
Palmer-Skok, Virginia, *Images of America (Arcadia Publishing , 2003)*
Rockey, John L., *History of New Haven County, Connecticut* (W. W. Preston, 1892)
Sharpe, William Carvosso, *South Britain Sketches and Records* (Record Print, 1898)

Primary Newspapers

Bridgeport Port, Bridgeport, Connecticut
Bridgeport Telegram, Bridgeport Connecticut
Danbury News-Times, Danbury, Connecticut
Hartford Courant, Hartford, Connecticut
New Haven Register-Courier, New Haven, Connecticut
New York Times, New York City, New York
Record-Journal, Meriden, Connecticut
Stamford Daily Advocate, Stamford, Connecticut
Waterbury Republican, Waterbury, Connecticut
Waterbury Democrat, Waterbury, Connecticut
Waterbury American, Waterbury, Connecticut

Online Sources

www.Genealogybank.com
www.NewsArchives.com
www.newspapers.com
www.southburyhistory.org
www.ushmm.org

Connecticut State Library, Archives Room, Wilbur Cross Papers, 1937-1938, Box #409, *Nazi Camp-Southbury Folder*
South Britain Congregational Church, *Bund Collection, Rev. Lindsay Letters*
Southbury Historical Society, Old Town Hall Museum, *Bund Collection*
Southbury Historical Society, Old Town Hall Museum, *Carol Hagy/Rev. Lindsay Scrapbook File*
United States Holocaust Memorial Museum, *Lindsay Collection*